CRACK THE CODE

UPGRADE YOUR CUSTOMER EXPERIENCE
ONE CONVERSATION AT A TIME

Blue Sky Performance Improvement
The Old Malt House
33 The Street
Shalford
Guildford
GU4 8BU

Tel : +44 1483 739400

Email: info@blue-sky.co.uk
Website: www.blue-sky.co.uk

First published in Great Britain in 2017 by Blue Sky

ISBN: 978-1-9997152-0-5

British Library cataloguing in Publication Data

A CIP catalogue record for this book can be obtained from the British Library

Cover and book design by Lewis Young

Set in Minion Pro and Helvetica

Printed by IQ Digital House

CRACK THE CODE

UPGRADE YOUR CUSTOMER EXPERIENCE
ONE CONVERSATION AT A TIME

Sally Earnshaw

Sean Spurgin & Steve Bent

CONTENTS

CHAPTER 1: MIND THE GAP

ONCE UPON AN IPAD

I have something to confess. I'm a bad mother.

I don't mean that in a self-critical or self-pitying way. I'm pretty certain that all mothers are rubbish, now and again. But I've recently been feeling my failings more strongly than usual, and it's all down to the bloody iPad.

I have three kids, the youngest of whom is four years old. He has an iPad (don't judge me). He loves it (don't judge him). But he still needs help to use some of the books and games. So, when we're all together at home on the weekends, I'll often hear him asking his older siblings for help with that special sort of persistence only four-year-olds have. Help me, help me, help me. Now, now, now.

Invariably, his brother and sister ignore him, their heads buried in devices of their own. The more he nags, the more they withdraw.

It drives him nuts.

Eventually, my youngest will give up on them and turn to me. I'm invariably trying to do at least four other things at the time: make a meal, text my partner, call my mum, finish a work email. Help me, help me, help me, now, now, now.

It drives me nuts. So, I'll grab the iPad and restart the game, or swap the book, or solve whatever the issue is as quickly as I can. Then I'll hand it back to him and get back to my juggling, trying to ignore the guilty little voice at the back of my mind.

I helped him, didn't I? I answered his question? I fixed his problem?

Of course not. But more about that later on.

THE GOOD NEWS

I assume, considering you're reading this book, that your job involves leading, shaping or delivering customer experience for your organisation in some way.

Congratulations: you won the career lottery. You're the hottest property in town.

Today, from the CEOs of big old blue chips to the founders of tiny niche startups, everyone seems to agree that customer experience is where it's at. Now that people can buy almost anything with one click, research almost anything with two, conduct an opinion poll with a couple of tweets and broadcast their opinions across the internet within seconds of a service or sales conversation, securing their love and loyalty as customers and brand advocates has never been more important.

The figures bear this out. From the LSE study showing that a 1 per cent uplift in a company's Net Promoter Score (NPS) is worth £9m[1], to the evidence that NPS leaders grow, on average, at more than twice the rate of their competitors,[2] a growing body of research demonstrates that deeply engaged customers are the secret weapon for businesses that want to thrive, or even just survive, in tough economic times.

No wonder, then, that the industry is booming. Four out of five people currently sit in sales and service roles in this country,[3] and there are 750,000 people working in contact centres right now, generating 42 billion minutes of inbound interactions a year.[4] And those are just the figures for the UK - imagine how many more billions of customer conversations are happening right now across the globe.

---

1 Customer Advocacy Drives UK Business Growth, 05 September 2005, Dr Paul Marsden, LSE
2 Bain and Co http://www.netpromotersystem.com/about/measuring-your-net-promoter-score.aspx
3 Resolution Foundation analysis of ONS statistics Q1 2017 http://www.bbc.co.uk/news/election-2017-39966615
4 http://www.contactbabel.com/pdfs/dec2014/uk%20soitp%202015%20marketing.pdf

But they're just the tip of the iceberg. In our new economy of the empowered consumer, customer experience is no longer just the job of the Customer Service director. Now that organisations have the opportunity to create relationships with their customers in so many different ways, it has become the responsibility of everybody in the business - from the cleaners right the way through to the Board - to maximise the value of every single point of customer contact. Whether you're on the shop floor, in the head office or on Twitter, you have to be ready to have a conversation with a customer anywhere, any time.

The fact is we *all* work in sales and service nowadays. So, this must be a golden age for customer experience, right? A utopia of warm, responsive people-first organisations and satisfied, loyal consumers?

Well, not quite.

THE BAD NEWS

There's a whole other set of figures that tells another side to this story.

For example, half of the brands on the Institute of Customer Service (ICS)'s UK best-for-service chart have remained the same for the last five years.[5] You can probably name most of them: Amazon, John Lewis, First Direct, Nationwide, M&S Food. In other words, for some reason, the companies that do this stuff well are still doing it well, but everyone else is still failing to nail that elusive service 'magic', even if their entire staff has been given the job of knocking it out of the park.

Then there's the research telling us that brands in the UK are currently losing nearly £15 billion annually due to poor customer service.[6] Or the survey that found that 89 per cent of consumers have stopped doing business with a company after experiencing poor

---

5 https://www.instituteofcustomerservice.com/research-insight/research-library/ukcsi-the-state-of-customer-satisfaction-in-the-uk-january-2017
6 Harris/ClickSoftware Survey http://www.prnewswire.com/news-releases/uk-businesses-losing-over-a-third-of-customers-due-to-poor-service-267117651.html

customer service.[7] And when we conducted our own survey into the state of UK sales and service at Blue Sky, we found that only 21 per cent of people described their customer experience as excellent, while 78 per cent declared that they would be willing to pay more for a better one.

This all paints a pretty bleak picture of the state of the nation's service.

The problem is there's a massive gap between having good intentions, and knowing how to turn those good intentions into actions that will result in lasting change. And I see this gap showing up time and again in my work with some of the UK's biggest companies.

If you gather 500 leaders of top FTSE 100 companies in a room and ask them to put their hands up if customer experience is high on their agenda, you'll see 500 hands in the air (I speak from personal experience here). If you ask those leaders a second question - can you describe a good customer experience? - you'll probably get another 500 waving palms. You'll also find a decent level of consensus in the room as to what a good customer experience looks like; we all know it when we see it, after all. But if you ask the same 500 leaders to raise their hands if they can describe what it is that best-for-service organisations do to create those good experiences over and over and over again, the hands start to waver, and the answers will be all over the shop. Some might say that it's all down to process. Some might talk about an inspiring vision. Some might enthuse about the latest technology they've installed.

Very, very rarely will you hear someone mention climate.

And that's where it's all going wrong.

7 Right Now Customer Experience Impact Report https://www.salesforce.com/blog/2013/08/customer-service-stats.html

A QUICK ASIDE

When I first started in the workplace twenty-five years ago, I was lucky enough to work for a very inspiring, customer-focused business. They had 'think of yourself as a customer' emblazoned above every door in gold letters, E-type jags in the lobby, apple trees… oh, it was just lovely. I even remember one of the quotes in the hall: "If our failure rate is one in ten thousand, what do we say to that one customer?" I was an advisor on the phones back then, and I really used to agonise: Yes! God! What do we say to that one customer? I bought into it all, one hundred per cent. I saw just how powerfully it motivated the staff, delighted the customers - and drove profit for the business, too.

It was only when I moved on that I realised this wasn't a truthful picture of the state of the nation's service. The disillusionment I experienced when I encountered other companies' attitude to their customers - not to mention their own people - bubbled up into a huge sense of disbelief and frustration. It was a painful fall from a lofty start. Thankfully, my anger quickly transformed into a fierce hunger to recreate that climate in all sorts of other businesses and sectors - a climate that consistently and visibly put people first.

For a while my LinkedIn bio stated that I was 'on a mission to change the nation's service'. I know that might sound a bit grand, a bit melodramatic, and for us Brits perhaps even a bit American (gosh!), but it is utterly true. I really do care about creating the best customer experience possible, because that challenge has an impact far beyond customer experience. It asks me, and the people I work with, to continually work on being more human: as bosses, as colleagues, hell, even as parents (as I said, more about that later on).

And no, it doesn't have to involve apple trees or E-types, but it does involve changing every conversation that happens across your organisation, every day, in order to create a climate where people and customer experience thrives. And I'm not going to lie: that's a massive undertaking. It's not easy.

But that's why it's a job worth doing. Worth dedicating your whole se
to.

TIME FOR AN UPGRADE

The problem with companies used to be that they put profit before
people. But that's not so much the case now. The new problem is that,
while organisations understand the importance of people, they don't
understand how to put them first.

Thankfully, there is an essentially simple solution. To create a climate
that values people before everything else, leaders need to invest in better
technology. It's just not the technology that they think.

Imagine for a moment that your CEO is being pitched a new piece of
enterprise-wide software by the founder of a Silicon Valley startup.
According to the twenty-something in the hoodie, this software is
responsible for the service and sales results of every one of the world's
best-in-class companies, from Waitrose to Zappos. The technology
is copyright-free, open source and compatible with all your existing
hardware. It comes with the most advanced AI ever invented, allowing it
to continually learn, adapt and improve. The more you use it, the better
it works. And it is not only guaranteed to skyrocket your customer
satisfaction and sales figures; it is proven to have a profound effect on
internal retention, loyalty and efficiency too. Finally, the pitch concludes,
if used correctly, this software even has the potential to transform your
personal health, happiness and relationships.

If the twenty-something in the hoodie had the data to back up his
claims, your CEO would be insane not to invest but, in this story that's
exactly what he doesn't do and that's exactly the scenario that plays out
in boardrooms across the UK every day. Because the technology we're
talking about here doesn't come from Silicon Valley, and it's more likely
to be pitched by a weary Head of Customer Experience or Operations
Director than a Californian code monkey.

L-powered computer code. It's human-powered

n Code ™. And although it has been around for a few

's currently undergoing a huge upgrade thanks to leaps

the fields of neuroscience, psychology, social anthropology

and behavioural economics.

That's the secret behind today's customer experience gap: to become a best-in-class company, you need to have smarter, better, more human conversations. Simple as that.

However, because it concerns people rather than ones and zeros, the art and science of good conversation is falling further and further down leaders' priority lists. Which is particularly unfortunate when you realise that it is exactly this obsession with impersonal technology that makes human conversation more valuable than ever before.

THE TANGIBILITY BIAS

In November 2016, the recruitment and consultancy giant Korn Ferry interviewed 800 CEOs of multimillion and multibillion-dollar global organisations on their views concerning the future of work.[8] Sixty-three per cent claimed that in five years, technology would be their firm's greatest source of competitive advantage. Sixty-seven per cent said that technology would create greater value in the future than people. Forty-four per cent said that the prevalence of robotics, automation and artificial intelligence would make people "largely irrelevant" over the coming decade.

When they compared these views with the actual data about the value people bring to an organisation, the researchers concluded that these leaders were falling prey to a dangerous, if all-too-human, psychological illusion. "Leaders may be facing what experts call a tangibility bias," declared Jean-Marc Laouchez, Korn Ferry's Global Managing Director of Solutions. "Facing uncertainty, they are putting priority in their thinking, planning and execution on the tangible – what they can see,

8 http://www.kornferry.com/institute/2030-the-very-human-future-of-work

touch and measure, such as technology investments. Putting an exact value on people is much more difficult, even though people directly influence the value of technology, innovation and products."

This tangibility bias is a phenomenon I've seen crop up time and again in organisations of all sizes and sectors over the years - and it's definitely getting worse. Because investing in people feels more complex and nebulous than buying a chunk of software, leaders are throwing money at everything except the one thing that counts.

People have conversations; conversations create climate; climate is what determines the success of your customer experience. That's the 'magic technology' that world-class service organisations use to stay ahead of their competitors, year after year. One big Board-level conversation might help, but it's not going to drive real change. Change comes from having hundreds of human conversations, at every level of the organisation, every day, one at a time.

And although that process is complex, it is in no way abstract. It is something you can learn.

GET READY TO WORK

Creating a climate where great customer experience thrives might be an art, but it's also an exact and replicable science. I have been lucky enough to work with those who do it best (and worst) for twenty-five years, observing and experimenting alongside thousands of sales and service leaders and frontline staff in hundreds of organisations across the world. And there is a method in the magic.

The big organisational thinkers of the twenty-first century such as Dan Pink, Simon Sinek, Adam Grant and Daniel Kahneman are all, in their various ways, pushing the same essential message: understand humans, help them have better conversations and make better decisions, and your business will lead the field. Their ideas certainly provide a brilliant backdrop when seeking the holy grail of best-in-class customer experience, and we'll reference their awesome work in the following chapters. But when you're working in the reality of sales and service every single day, it's vital to translate the theory into action too.

How can you give your Board a clear roadmap to improvement, backed by data, in order to secure investment in your people, not just your tech? What seven behaviours will help your service and sales people have the sort of conversations that will blow their super-informed customers away? Which five mindsets will ensure that your customer experience doesn't just improve in the short term, but will earn you a place on the ICS index for years to come? What one thing can you personally do on Monday morning to start the process of turning your company's climate into one that truly puts people first?

That's what you'll find in this book. A manual, not a manifesto. With the help of hundreds of colleagues and clients, I've filtered the big scientific ideas through real experience, real companies and real people to close the gap between intention and action, and help you build a climate that will deliver real results.

The world may have gone gaga for Google, but human conversations remain your most valuable code. Learn how to create the climate for customer experience to thrive every day, and you won't just change how good you are at your job, how much you love your job, and how much money your organisation makes.

You might just start to change your life. Are you ready to start?

CHAPTER 2: SETTING THE TONE

BRIEF ENCOUNTER

Recently, one of my colleagues Carol travelled up to Manchester on the train for a meeting. She sat opposite a young woman, who was hammering away on her laptop, and settled down to hammer away at hers. However, after a while, Carol noticed that there was a sticker on her fellow passenger's laptop lid: *Work Hard. Have Fun. Make History.* Carol loved it. She wanted one. So, she asked the young woman where it came from.

The young woman explained that she was a Procurement Officer for Amazon Logistics and, without any prompting, launched into a compelling story about Amazon. She explained why those particular words had been chosen by Jeff Bezos as the company's internal motto, how they were brought to life by leaders inside the business and how she personally strove to make them show up in her work every day. She ended up chatting to Carol for over an hour about what she did, how she did it and how she felt. She gave precise examples of the great work her department had achieved and the ways in which they continued to innovate. This young woman really was the living embodiment of Amazon's slogan, and she insisted that the same applied across the vast organisation of which she was a proud part.

Ever since Carol told me that story, I can't help but look at the nondescript brown parcels that arrive on my doorstep almost every week in an entirely different way.

TUNING UP

Mission. Purpose. Vision. Philosophy. Excuse me while I throw up.

Could these be the most irritating words in the business world? They promise so much, yet deliver so little. "We inspire the human spirit" might look great mounted in neon cathodes on your office wall, and a 126-page values deck might go down a storm at a conference, but it can all sound pretty meaningless to a service rep knee-deep in their twentieth angry customer conversation of the day.

However, Just because most companies fail to live up to their vision, that doesn't mean you don't need one. You really do. Every business needs to define their ethos, which is the term we use to describe what you stand for in terms of customer experience. Best-for-service businesses always have one and manage to achieve a sort of 'ethos alchemy'. They somehow manage to turn words about what they stand for into a living, breathing climate that touches their customers in all sorts of concrete and memorable ways.

IRL: THE SMILE HIGH CLUB

At any given time during a trip with Southwest Airlines, their service reminds you you're flying with them. Their friendly demeanour and tennis shoes - at the counter, at the gate, on the plane - are all signals you're with Southwest. The humour they employ - at the gate, over the in-flight intercom and in their wonderful commercials - reminds you you're partnering with the fun folks at Southwest. That's their service ethos and it's memorable, meaningful and profitable. It's more than just peanuts.

Yep, we've stumbled upon that bloody gap again. The gap between good intentions and knowing how to put those good intentions into practice. But now I'm going to introduce you to the first tool that will help you leap across it.

It's called tone.

Tone is at the top of the customer experience transformation tree. Set the right tone, and it will nurture the right climate, which will then drive the right conversations and result in the right customer experience. Get it wrong and however much time and effort you put into training skills, behaviours and mindsets, they just won't 'take'.

Tone isn't your strategy. It isn't what you do, or how you do it. Tone is all about who you are. But it's not just the promise about who you are as an organisation; it's what that promise feels and smells and looks like. It's the sound of that promise, playing out in conversations across your business every day. And it comes from the very highest levels of leadership.

MAKING SOUNDWAVES

Tone comes from the top, as in founder, owner, board. 'Top down' leadership might have become unfashionable but when it comes to tone, nothing else works.

It's so easy to think that 'being customer-focused' is the job of the front line staff, because they're the ones having the direct conversations with customers every day. But to create a climate where those conversations can reach their full potential, the customer has to be at the heart of every decision your leadership team makes, every process your operational guys design, even the language you use within the boardroom. How many conversations are your senior leaders having about media, channels, data, interactions, metrics... and how many about customers? Next time you have a leadership meeting, try counting the number of times the words 'customer' and 'people' show up. It can be a pretty sobering exercise.

IRL: PUTTING THE CUSTOMER IN THE BOARDROOM

In one company we know, there's a cardboard cut-out of a 'customer' in every meeting room to remind leaders who they're talking about. In another, they leave a chair empty at the head of every table to represent the customer's influence on everything they do. In a third, they insist that everyone spells Customer with a capital C. These are just small examples, but they make a big difference. They set the tone for a customer-focused business, right from the very top.

So, setting the right tone means putting the customer first, right from the very top. But that doesn't mean you're exempt from reading this chapter if you're not the CEO. Although it's important for those head honchos to set the tuning fork quivering, it's everyone's responsibility to keep that note resonating throughout the business.

In a paper for Harvard Business Review[9] which later developed into
a bestselling book, Stanford Professor Debra Meyerson championed
a new sort of leader she dubbed 'tempered radicals'. "Research has
shown that organisations change primarily in two ways: through drastic
action and through evolutionary adaptation," she writes. "In the former
case, change is discontinuous and often forced on the organisation or
mandated by top management in the wake of technological innovations,
by a scarcity or abundance of natural resources, or by sudden changes
in the regulatory, legal, competitive or political landscape. Under
such circumstances, change may happen quickly and often involves
significant pain. Evolutionary change, by contrast, is gentle, incremental,
decentralised, and over time produces a broad and lasting shift with less
upheaval."

Meyerson believes that the people who lead the second sort of change
are not protestors with placards, but dedicated individuals finding a way
to create ripples in their own modest circles of influence. "They exercise
a form of leadership within organisations that is more localised, more
diffuse, more modest, and less visible than other forms - yet no less
significant."

We all have the power - indeed, the duty - to be tempered radicals, if we
want the status quo to change. Everyone's at the top of some sphere of
influence, even if it's a small one. If you're a line manager, it's your job to
set the tone for your direct reports. If you're a team leader, it's your job
to set the tone for your group. So how do you do it?

To set the tone you need to know what you stand for, commit to making
Symbolic Acts, and create a permission culture.

Let's break it down, and get to work.

---

9 https://sites.stanford.edu/tempered-radicals/sites/default/files/hbr-tr.pdf

1. KNOW WHAT YOU STAND FOR

To really know what you stand for as a business, you need to equip yourself with three tools: one ethos, a sprinkling of service principles and lots of stories.

First, establish your ethos

Historically, the service industry has behaved a bit like a shoal of fish. In the early days of retail, service was all about quality; companies competed to prove that they provided the highest quality experience, the sort that made shopping at a department store feel like an event and evoked the personal attention customers were used to receiving in local shops. With the rise of consumer regulation legislation and consumer advocacy organisations such as Which? in the 1980s, the emphasis shifted to standards, and companies rushed to prove that they were ticking all the right boxes and provide guarantees. Then in the 1990s, the landscape shifted again to prioritise surprise and delight, and 'wowing' the customer; I can't tell you how many books I read with titles involving that damn three-letter word.

But the rise of the digital economy in the twenty-first century has acted like a shark, scattering the consensus and forcing each company to identify how they stand out from - not keep up with - the crowd.

So, on one hand we have Marks & Spencer, which has been steadily offering its "no quibble guarantee" for decades, and which ensures that promise is ingrained into every employee brain, customer touchpoint and customer experience across its stores. If you snag the sleeve of your new M&S top and take it back to the store, you can look the lady at the returns desk in the eyeballs and know that she knows it's not the first time you've worn that top, but also know that she's going to take it back, even though she knows exactly what you've done. And although that might not be admirable (and this is an *entirely* hypothetical scenario, of course), when the customer knows your ethos as well as you do, and knows they can rely on it to work, you're doing something very right. Then, there's the American clothing company Zappos, which has taken

a t-shirt. For example, one company I came across had the values 'Be Proud! Be Ingenious! Be Green!' I have no idea how you would translate pride, ingenuity or greenness into a customer experience and, frankly, I have no desire to find out.

One of my little obsessions (I have a few) involves testing whether a company's ethos really does carry through in all of its packaging and marketing, not to mention the behaviour of its front line customer service teams. All too often, the rhetoric just doesn't stack up with the reality; however, from time to time, I do come across a company that absolutely gets it right.

One of my favourites is Innocent, the smoothie brand. I have no idea whether Innocent has service principles or brand values, but I can tell you what they do have: a warm, light-hearted and human spirit that shows up in everything they do. This is obviously a brand that is crystal clear on what it stands for, and that has articulated that ethos internally in a way that reaches the front line. Here's an example of an email exchange I fabricated with them to test out their company ethos.

✉ Mail

From: Sally Earnshaw
To: 'Innocent Smoothies'
Subject: Enquiry

Hi there,

I am writing to check in as to the suitability of Innocent smoothies for babies. My littlest won't let my older two swig their smoothies without wanting some himself and if we don't let him he goes mental. I know it says only fruit, but I never believe what I read on the packaging. Supermarkets have a habit of lying to customers and I am not keen on putting anything unsuitable in to my baby's diet.

I'd be really interested in your thoughts.

Thanks
Sally Earnshaw

From: 'Innocent Smoothies'
To: Sally Earnshaw
Subject: RE: Enquiry

Hello Sally

Thank you for your email - I quite understand that you want to be certain about what goes into your little ones' mouths. I feel just the same with my little boy.

However, I can assure you that all of our smoothies are made of 100% pure fruit and absolutely nothing else. However, this does come with a BUT for children under 36 months and I have given you all of the information below so that you can make up your own mind. I do give smoothies to my little one (18 months) but at least you will have all the information to make an informed decision:

With everything we make we have to err on the side of caution as the last thing we want is for someone to become ill from one of our products. All our products are 100% natural and, as such, are dependent on the elements. Some fruits, in this case apples, contain micro bugs that aren't suitable for younger stomachs. The weather conditions last season meant that our suppliers couldn't guarantee our usual level of bugs and so, to be prudent, we've put this warning on our fruit tubes to make sure that we look after those little ones, with more sensitive stomachs than us. As I mentioned before, children under 36 months have very sensitive stomachs and there is a stricter limit for them, within food production, about what they should eat. The tubes are completely fine for children over the age of 36 months.

Please rest assured that the level of bugs in our fruit tubes is still well within all normal levels and legislation and is nothing to be concerned about.

None of this is said to scare you - but we just want to ensure that our products are doing people good.

I hope this helps to explain things more to you.
All the best,
Jenny

My point is does what you stand for translate through to the front line? For Innocent, it absolutely does.

The fast-growing online fashion retailer Asos also has a clear set of values this time tied to its vision of relentless and aggressive innovation. "At Asos, people push things forward," the company declares.[11] "We're authentic, brave and creative in everything we do. We wouldn't be where we are today without embracing those values. When we say retail doesn't get much faster than this, we mean it. From our designers and photographers to customer advisors and technology specialists, we're entrepreneurs from top to bottom. We're forever pushing boundaries and breaking barriers in our quest to be first in everything we do. In fact, we want to be the world's number one fashion retailer. So, we're ambitious. And we mean business."

Asos has three values, and personally I'm a big fan of three. Why? Well, there are no hard and fast rules here - Zappos has ten and Blue Sky has one (Be The Best You Can Be) but generally I find three principles are enough to explain what you stand for, but not so many that they won't slip out of the brain of even the most exhausted sales rep (or indeed CEO). When you have maybe 5000, 10,000 or 20,000 people in your business, aiming for more than three principles seems a little bit mad to me (be honest - can you really remember all seven of Stephen Covey's effective habits?!). And considering that the 'rule of three' has proved its worth in everything from jazz to religion to comedy writing, it's a pretty safe bet.

But this isn't an exact science. Whether you opt for three or thirteen service principles, the important thing here is to identify exactly how your ethos looks and feels in terms of customer experience - in a few specific, practical and memorable ways.

IRL: THERE ARE PRINCIPLES, THEN THERE ARE PRINCIPLES

I was lucky enough to interview Bob Chapman, CEO and Chairman of technology solutions firm Barry-Wehmiller and founder of the Truly Human Leadership approach. I asked Bob about how he managed to stick to his own service principles when times got tough, and he told me this story. It blew me away.

"What happened in 2008-9, we had developed our guiding principles; I was flying around the world talking about it: 'we care for the lives of the people we touch'," Bob explained. "I was preaching and all of a sudden the economic downturn hit in October, and in January I walked into a Board meeting and the first thing they said to me was: 'Don't you think you need to lay off some people? We're in the middle of the worst downturn.'

"I said 'No I don't think so' - we had good backlogs, we were okay financially. Then one and a half months later I was in Italy, and a major customer just put on hold a major order that we had, a multimillion-dollar order, and I said 'Oh my God! It's hit us! What are we going to do?' So I thought about our guiding principle - we measure success by the way we touch the lives of people - so I said to myself, if we lay off people we're going to hurt some people. We can't hurt people. So because I'd been preaching it, and because we believe what we articulate, I said:

'We can't do this. What would a caring family do if a member of the family was impacted dramatically by something? We would all pitch in and take a little pain so that our family member wouldn't take a lot of pain.'

"So in that thought process I came up with an idea that I had never heard of before, which was the idea of furloughs: if we all took a month off without pay, so that no-one had to be let go. The reaction was phenomenal. Everybody was scared to death for their job and, when we said we're not going to let people go, the people who took the time off didn't see it as a method of improving the profitability of the company - they saw it as a gesture to help their friends not lose their job in the company. And they were so proud.

"And we allowed them to take their month off when they could be with family or parents or children, so it was a bonus. They gave up one twelfth of their income and our culture took a dramatic step forward. Who you are in your worst of times is who you are, not you in your best of times. We didn't let people go, and nine to twelve months later things started to improve and things started to get better and our company exploded up. Unless you articulate what you believe, how do you make any decision, without some framework of your beliefs?"

⚡ CRACK THE CODE: DEFINE YOUR SERVICE PRINCIPLES

Service principles set a clear direction for everyone in the business. The strength of each principle lies in its clarity of purpose and how translatable it is to front line teams. Strong service principles are a powerful way to get your people out of their silos and see the bigger picture. Built on customer insight, they convey fundamental truths that unite and inspire teams, enabling them to deliver certain outcomes even when processes and systems are not aligned. They also enable managers to drive consistent service delivery, ultimately making life simpler for customers and the business.

So now take your ethos and break it down into three promises you make your customers about the sort of service they can expect, based on customer insight. These can be both customer-facing ('we make them feel this way') and internally focused ('we do it this way').

Then create three stories for each service principle, illustrating how each one might play out in a real situation for both customers and employees (think of Bob Chapman's amazing example above).

Now, find your compelling story

"If you want to learn about a culture listen to the stories. If you want to change a culture, change the stories." This old adage might sound obvious but, when you really start to explore it, you realise how powerful it really is. Because once you're clear on your ethos and service principles, you need to share them - and the most effective way to share what you stand for is through stories.

Stories are our oldest technology. Since Homo sapiens first sat around campfires eating roast mammoth, we've been using the same basic five-act story structure[12] to sell our fellow humans on everything from fairy tales to Pixar cartoons[13] to any episode of *House of Cards*.

Stories help us feel a part of something larger than ourselves, give us a sense of purpose, and smuggle beliefs and information into our brains in an emotive and memorable way. In other words, they're naturally viral.

So, if you want to establish a compelling shared story about who you are as an organisation, it helps to use this primal tech already embedded in our brains. When applied to organisations, the archetypal five-act story structure plays out like this:

1. What's changing around us that's driving a need to up our game?
2. Where are we now as a business/division/team?
3. What's our big idea? What do we stand for?

12 Into The Woods: How Stories Work and Why We Tell Them, John Yorke, Penguin, April 2014
13 https://www.khanacademy.org/partner-content/pixar/storytelling

4. What's it going to take from our leaders and our people?
5. What behaviours need to show up every day?

All you need to do is take your business and your market and shape it into this story, in a way that makes sense to you. And before you panic: this doesn't mean you have to become a Pixar-level 'storyteller'. You don't have to start going to open mic spoken-word sessions or take expensive courses (there are a lot of them about). As we've seen, storytelling is the most natural and instinctive human behaviour there is. Trust me: you're *already* an expert. All you need to do is be really clear on your story, believe in what you're saying - and make the time to share.

IRL: FROM STRUGGLE TO STORY

One of our clients, a global telco company, went on an amazing journey of transformation that hinged on its leadership team discovering and then sharing their compelling story.

By getting together and properly digging down into how the world was changing around them, they finally understood why they were struggling to keep their customers satisfied. On the one hand, they had tech-savvy customers demanding to always be seamlessly connected, with all their telephone and internet and hardware needs served in an effortless one-stop shop; on the other, they had an equal number of customers who barely understood how their mobile billing worked. They also needed to adapt to the fact that competitors had really raised the bar in terms of service, and how the increasing regionalisation of government was impacting on customers' expectations and market behaviour.

Despite all their good intentions, they realised that most of their customers were apathetic and indifferent towards their brand. As a leadership team, they'd invested too much time in improving internal processes rather than focusing on the moment-to-moment experience for their customers.

The big idea that emerged from these insights was simple, like all the best ones are: they needed to have better conversations, one at a time. They acknowledged that all of their customers had unique and specific aspirations - whether they were struggling to start a small business or aiming for the stars - and that it was only by being curious, by getting to know them and predicting what they needed before they knew they needed it, that the company could turn them into advocates. They had to over-deliver, live the principles... and unquestioningly up their game.

The leadership team broke the story down into a clear storybook, complete with defined service principles. Then they recruited their front line teams to be part of the story, asking them to actively test out these ideas, to challenge them and report back. The result was a workforce that was hugely re-energised and customer satisfaction ratings that began to climb. Using the power of a compelling story, the company's leaders had turned what had seemed to be an intransigent challenge into an inspiring rallying call.

CRACK THE CODE: FIND YOUR COMPELLING STORY

Get a pen (I find old-fashioned ink and paper works best for this sort of thinking) and write a page or so for each story 'act' as it applies to your business, customers and industry. It's important not to skip a step, and to complete each one before moving on to the next.

Ask your colleagues on the leadership team to draft their own versions in parallel. When you come together you'll be able to compare, contrast and discuss. It's fine (in fact essential) to each have your own personal take on the story - but it's also important to make sure that they all share the same basic facts, end vision and overall ethos.

Next, share it - again, and again, and again

At this point you may well be thinking: but we already have an ethos and a story! I can recite it verbatim! Everyone in this place knows what we stand for! Our service principles are everywhere!

In which case, it's time to test that we're not suffering from 'the curse of knowledge'.

This phenomenon came to light in 1990, thanks to a study by a Stanford University graduate psychology student named Elizabeth Newton.[14] Newton set up a simple experiment in which she assigned people to one of two roles: 'tapper' or 'listener'. Each tapper was asked to pick a well-known song, such as 'Happy Birthday', and tap out the rhythm on a table; the listener's job was to guess the song. Before they started each time, Newton asked the tappers to predict the probability that listeners would correctly guess their song. The tappers predicted 50 per cent. But over the course of the experiment, 120 songs were tapped out, and listeners guessed only three of the songs correctly: a woeful strike rate of 2.5 per cent.

How could Newton explain this gap between the expectations of the tappers and the behaviour of the listeners? Newton concluded that when a tapper tapped, it was impossible for them to avoid 'hearing' the tune accompanying their taps. All the listeners heard was an abstract code, but the tappers found it hard to believe that they couldn't somehow overhear the silent tune playing out in their own heads. In other words, once we know something, we find it hard to imagine not knowing it. We have difficulty sharing it with others, because we can't readily recreate their 'innocent' state of mind. Just play a game of Pictionary or Charades with your family at Christmas, and you'll understand exactly what Newton's getting at.

So, don't make assumptions when it comes to sharing your compelling story. Imagine that no-one has heard anything like it before, and that it's

---

14 https://hbr.org/2006/12/the-curse-of-knowledge;at/1

your job to embed it in the brains of everyone around you. How? This one's simple. Just tell it: again, and again, and again.

I learned the 'tappers and listeners' lesson myself the hard way, when I first took on the MD role at Blue Sky. A few months into the gig I planned on writing a blog called 'Leadership lessons from a new MD' focused just on this topic of how unbelievably bloody hard it is to communicate a new story about what you stand for (of course, I've still not got around to writing it!). The essence of my experience was: you think you've communicated something, you've told the whole company, you've sat in meetings, you've sent around emails, you've followed up ... and no matter how thorough you've been, there is always one person who you then find out says that they don't know! It's so hard to get it right. And the only way to get it right is to keep on repeating yourself over and over and over again, and accept that that is what you have to do. And not get frustrated. It's not because other people haven't listened, it's just human nature. Stories don't go in straight away.

One of my favourite ever clients, Andrew Reaney - now MD at British Gas - expressed this brilliantly when he told me, "You've just got to become a stuck record." Normally in life that's seen as a bad thing but, when it comes to your compelling story, you really do want to emulate a piece of scratched old vinyl stuttering over the same few bars.
Bored of the sound of your own voice? Step it up. Go on overdrive. Share that story even more.

 ## IRL: FROM TAPPERS TO RAPPERS

Remember the story you just read about the global telco company that found their compelling story by turning their toughest challenges into an inspiring rallying call?

Well, before leaving the event, one team leader even turned the story into a rap, so that he could share the message with his team in a way he thought would resonate. He recorded a video on his phone as he was on his four-hour journey back from the venue and distributed the clip.

I love this guy. He embodied the story that we'd told. It was shameless, it was exposing, it was mad, it was genius - and it had the most incredible impact.

 # LEADERSHIP HACKS: STORYTELLING

Having a compelling, revolution-inspiring story is no good if only six people in a room on the tenth floor know what it is. You need to do more than just etch it on the glass of your conference room. Here are five things you can do to rally people around it right now.

i) Know your why
Be clear in your own mind why your people should join you in the revolution. Write down why you personally care about becoming a customer-first organisation. What makes you passionate about it? Give five reasons why it will make things better for everyone.

ii) Find your authenticity
To tell a great business story, it's important to be authentic. The best storytellers look to their own memories and life experiences for ways to illustrate their message. What events in your life make you believe in the idea you are trying to share? Write down some stories that tell other people more about who you are and why you're here. Don't be too afraid to tell stories that show failure, poor judgement, or mistakes on your part. When you're prepared to appear vulnerable in front of others, you can quickly establish trust and rapport. So, don't hide behind an email or a slide deck; find a bank of metaphors and real world examples you can share.

iii) Keep it simple
Not every story you tell has to be a surprising, edge-of-your-seat epic. Some of the most successful and memorable stories are relatively simple and straightforward. Don't let needless details detract from your core message. Work from the principle that 'less is more'. Commit to finding five simple, one-sentence stories from your work today that illustrate your cause and your ethos.

iv) Make it viral

Stories can change the way we think, act and feel. They form the foundations of an entire workplace culture, and they have the power to break down barriers and turn bad situations around. Stories can capture our imaginations, illustrate our ideas, arouse our passions and inspire us in a way that cold, hard facts often can't. So, don't assume everyone has got it - think 'tappers and listeners' – and help your story cascade. Coach others on how to create their version of the story, and you'll help it travel like wildfire.

v) Intentional practice

Storytelling is an art form that requires repeated effort to get right. Rehearse your story before you tell it, in the mirror or on your phone. Doing this just once can improve your storytelling beyond belief.

2. SYMBOLIC ACTS: DO SOMETHING SYMBOLIC

Now your compelling story is out there, being shared, you have to decide on the actions you're going to take to show that it's a documentary, not a fairy tale. That's right, you can't just work out how you're going to talk about your ethos and your service principles; you have to find ways in which you're going to *demonstrate* commitment to them. You have to story*do*, as well as story*tell*.

And by you, I mean *you*, and every one of your leadership colleagues. Symbolic Acts are purposefully designed to show that the leaders in your organisation have broken out of the ivory tower for good and are, from now onwards, going to consistently role-model the commitment to the customer they want to see show up in everyone else.

Scary? Yes. Effective? You bet. In one organisation I know, the higher up the food chain you are, the further away from the building you park, thus demonstrating that front line people are more important than the senior execs. Often, when I share that example with leaders, they'll say "er, I'm not sure about that one - have you got anything else??!" They don't tend to like that one! How about this: in another company I've worked with, every single person at every level of the business deals directly with customers, either by taking calls or working in stores, every single month. And if they don't demonstrate that they can deal with customers, they don't get promoted - whatever their role or seniority. Pretty powerful, right?

Remember Carol's neighbour on the train, with her effortless examples of how Amazon's ethos comes to life within the business? That's what happens when you have an organisation with cast-iron Symbolic Acts. Symbolic Acts become things that people in a business can talk about things that they are able to name-check as evidence that their leaders are personally committed to their customer approach. They're not just actions, they're mini-stories, and they can help to make your company's ethos more viral - not just internally but amongst the wider public too.

However, to qualify as a true Symbolic Act, these actions must display four characteristics. They must:

1. be visible
2. be consistent
3. be repeatable
4. and involve an element of sacrifice.

'Undercover operations' where CEOs secretly return to the shop floor for a year might make good TV, but they only really prove that no-one on the shop floor recognises their CEO's face. One-off gimmicks to foster company spirit with no auditing or accountability are the organisational equivalent of the boy who cried wolf. The truth is no-one really wants to take customer calls on top of their usual workload, serve customers on the frontline or walk an extra few minutes through the car park. But unless your Symbolic Acts hurt - just a bit, in a good way - they won't be powerful enough to truly set the tone.

Ready to decide on your own Symbolic Acts? We're going to split this exercise into four phases to make sure they really do fulfil all the criteria of a meaningful Symbolic Act. So, gather your leadership team together and get ready to challenge each other, be inspired by our real-life examples - and even try to have (gasp) fun!

⚡ CRACK THE CODE: MAKE YOUR SYMBOLIC ACTS VISIBLE

Next time you've got your senior leaders in a room, brainstorm five actions that you could all commit to doing that will demonstrate your customer philosophy in action. Ask yourselves:

- What's the most visible thing we could do to show that customers come before targets?
- How can we turn our service principles into things we can see, hear, touch and smell?
- What could we do to make our people do a double-take when they walked into the office on Monday morning?
- What things do we do that already reflect our ethos, and how can we bring more attention to them?

IRL: WALKING THE TALK

The American clothing company Zappos is a master of the art of the Symbolic Act. I recently interviewed their Head of People Operations, Hollie Delaney, and was blown away by the Symbolic Acts that their leaders have committed to, to bring their ten service principles to life.

For example, every single new starter in the business, top-level leaders as well as interns, goes through the full three-week frontline induction programme, because understanding the customer lies at the heart of everything they do. Another Symbolic Act is that every month, their finance division commits to walking around the organisation performing random acts of kindness. This doesn't just demonstrate Zappos' story that people are always their priority - it gives the CFO a chance to demonstrate that number-crunchers are human beings too.

It's impossible to visit Zappos HQ in Las Vegas without noticing these leader-led Symbolic Acts going on. They're talking points. They're small acts of theatre. They're on show.

🗲 CRACK THE CODE: MAKE YOUR SYMBOLIC ACTS REPEATABLE

In your leadership group, now look through the list of Symbolic Acts you've just created and ask how often they might occur.

- What can you do every year?
- Every month?
- Every week?
- Every day?

If you have gaps in these timescales, brainstorm some actions to fill them, remembering that they must be visible as well as consistent.

IRL: MUCK-IN MONDAY NIGHTS

A couple of years ago, a global credit card company went on a massive drive for acquisitions. Of course, this was also going to create a massive capacity issue for its already over-worked teams.

But instead of hiring temps, who would be expensive and would have no investment in the company culture, all the managers were sent to a briefing and trained on how to make credit decisions. Every Monday from 6pm to 10pm, without fail, they would order in pizza, sit together, and clear the backlog of credit decisions. Monday nights became credit nights, and you know what? They became the most efficient, energised time of the working week.

By creating this consistent habit, the company didn't just solve an acquisitions problem. It set the tone of how it approached its customers in an incredibly visible way, right from the top.

⚡ CRACK THE CODE: MAKE YOUR SYMBOLIC ACTS CONSISTENT

Now you need to ask yourselves how you're going to make sure these actions show up consistently, without fail.

- How will you share stories and examples, so people can see what others are doing?
- How are you going to hold each other accountable?
- What kind of alarms or trip wires might you be able to use to help keep you doing your Symbolic Acts? What new apps or mobile tech might you use?
- Can you anchor your Acts to particular times or places to make them easy to remember?

IRL: BOARD ROOM

Semco Partners, a Brazilian company best known for its radical form of industrial democracy and corporate re-engineering, keeps two chairs free at every one of its Board meetings. Those chairs are taken by the first two colleagues to arrive (there's often a queue for this opportunity) and each of those colleagues have the same opportunity to participate and the same voting rights as every senior executive at the meeting. As Ricardo Semler, who founded the company and personally champions the approach, says: "It keeps us honest."

⚡ CRACK THE CODE: MAKE YOUR SYMBOLIC ACTS HURT

Finally, ask yourselves as a leadership team:

- What do leaders in this company really not want to do?
- What would surprise people and get them saying "Wow, they really mean business this time?"
- If we could listen in on the gossip from our front line staff, what would they say we would never do in a million years?

- How could we bring to life what it feels like to be a dissatisfied customer of ours?
- What do we think people in this place would be willing to sacrifice to give the customer a better experience?

Now take these ideas and combine them with the list you already have. This should enable you to build your master list of Symbolic Acts - only actions that are highly visible, consistent and require an element of sacrifice are allowed to make the cut.

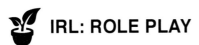 IRL: ROLE PLAY

Bruce Poon Tip, the founder of tour operator G Adventures, dropped the title of CEO (Chief Executive Officer) as he wanted to make sure that it was not considered the most important position in the company. To his mind, the most important position in the company is the customer-facing employee. Therefore, every single customer-facing employee in G Adventures has the title Chief Experience Officer (CEO). That's hundreds of CEOs, all with one singular responsibility: exceptional customer experience.

3. CREATE A PERMISSION CULTURE

So, now that you're clear on what you stand for and you've got a powerful arsenal of Symbolic Acts to bring it to life, it's time to take our third and final step in setting the tone. It's time to create a permission culture. And I have to admit, this can be a very tough step for leaders to take.

Giving permission is scary, but it really is one of those things that separates average customer experience from the amazing kind. That's because process only accounts for 80 to 90 per cent of what's required in a sales and service job. It's the 10 to 20 per cent of grey, the space for something personal and flexible, that allows your front line staff to truly put your customers' needs first. But they need your permission if they're going to make it work.

We all have experience of this. We can all think of a time when something has gone horribly wrong and we ring the call centre or walk into a store and we just want the person on the other end of the line to do the right thing and push process to one side. And we can all think of a time when they don't, because a true permission culture is a rare and beautiful beast.

Let me tell you a story that demonstrates this all too well. Recently, I was sitting with the leadership team of a white goods company, listening in to customer calls, when we got a call from a customer with five children who had a broken washing machine. As anybody with more than one kid will understand, this was a hands-down red-alert crisis! The customer had ordered a replacement machine a few days ago but, when she'd placed the order, she'd explained that there was a three-minute window during which she had to do the school run every day, and she had asked for the delivery team to avoid that time.

Unfortunately, she told us, she was on her way back from the school run when the delivery man rang her mobile from outside her house. She'd begged him to wait for two minutes but, with 16 visits to do that day, he had apologised and driven off. The customer saw the van pass as she was driving down the road and, with bags of stinking gym kit waiting to be washed on her back seat, had done a U-turn and followed it (while she spoke, this was all playing out in my head like some sort of action-movie car-chase!). When the van stopped at a light, our woman got out of her car, banged on the window (you go, girl!) and begged the delivery guy for the machine. The delivery man apologised again, but explained that the situation fell outside of process, so she would have to ring the call centre.

So here we were, with this poor desperate woman on the phone telling us her story, and the entire leadership team listening in. Of course, as mothers, as fathers - hell, as human beings - we were all rooting for her and longing for the call handler, Sarah, to find a way to get our heroine her washing machine. But we listened with sinking hearts as, in a very polite, professional and friendly manner, Sarah said: "I'm really sorry, but I have to do what the process tells me, which is to go for the next available delivery in ten days' time."

Look, there are no villains in this story. Sarah really was doing her best, within the constraints of her process. And I'm not saying that process isn't important. I'm a big fan of process. Companies like Amazon Logistics have a lot of very smart processes that help them deliver the great experience they do. But in that 10 to 20 per cent of time that you need to do something different, what separates the best from the rest is permission culture - knowing how far you can go for the customer when the situation dictates that you break the process, ignore the process or just find another process that hasn't been invented yet.

Let's go back to the room where we've gathered those 500 leaders, the ones in charge of top FTSE 100 companies. Ask them "Do your people have permission?" and all 500 of those hands will be thrusting into the air. But leave the room, get in your car and do a little tour of those leaders' front line staff, and I can guarantee that, with a handful of exceptions, their answer will be very different.

LEADERSHIP HACKS: GIVE PERMISSION

It might be scary, but as leaders we need to learn to let go. Giving permission might not be as bad as you think. It won't be like letting the lunatics run the asylum! We need to trust people to do the right thing, but this is a smart, not an indiscriminate, trust.

Our role is to support people to make the right choices, not control those choices all the time. It is about allowing people to make mistakes, and learn from them rather than chastise them. If you want employees to feel empowered to assist customers in creative ways, the moment you reprimand a single employee for 'doing something wrong', every other employee will then revert to their previous, timid ways, and never go out of their way for a customer again. But it is also about holding people to account for outcomes and the decisions they make.

We are all accountable to each other. We have a shared responsibility. That's the spirit you're looking for, and it thrives in the space between total freedom and overbearing control.

One reason that a permission culture is so rare is because leaders are often afraid it will lead to broken processes, inappropriate behaviour, spiralling costs, longer customer conversations, missed targets… in a word, anarchy. But that absolutely won't happen if those leaders take responsibility for modelling and articulating what a good permission culture looks like. And that begins with bookends.

First, establish your bookends

A couple of years ago, when I was staying in Scotland for a client workshop, I left one of my bags at my hotel. It wasn't until I got to the airport after the workshop that I realised I had left the bag behind. Panicked (my favourite jacket was in there!), I called the hotel. Without pausing to ask permission, the receptionist I spoke to fetched my bag, called a taxi, deposited a porter inside with my bag and sent it to the airport before my flight left. It was an amazing example of how far a company was willing to go to keep their customers happy.
Would you go that far? Further?

One of our clients, a national bank, told me another story that brilliantly demonstrated how far their permission culture stretched. A customer of theirs arrived at Leeds station only to discover that she'd lost her wallet on the train. Unable to get off the platform without a ticket but without any money to buy a new one, she realised she was stuck and rang the bank. As it happened, the bank's HQ was just around the corner from the station. The call handler got up from his desk, ran down to the station, got out some cash out from his own account and bought the customer a ticket.

Would you go that far? Further?

Or not so far?

Because it's also okay to have limits. The important thing is to establish exactly where those limits lie.

A good example here comes from a nationwide delivery service I recently worked with, who were anxious about establishing the right bookends for their business. Together, we discussed a scenario where an old lady goes to pick up a heavy parcel from a collection point. The parcel hasn't arrived yet, but it's due to come in on the next delivery. The guy serving the lady lives locally, he knows her, and his bus home goes right past her house. His instincts tell him that the right thing to do would be to take the parcel with him on the bus that night and drop it off. But while that would be a lovely judgement, it would also go against all this company's health and safety rules. For one thing, they don't know what's in the package. What if it was dangerous? What if he dropped it? What if it got stolen? What if the lady didn't answer her door?

As it turned out, the very act of articulating and sharing these worries within the leadership team solved them. Working through the story together allowed them to set their parameters for permission, in a way that was real and relatable. Once their frontline staff understood not just where the bookends sat but why, they found it easy to make the right judgements on their own.

CRACK THE CODE: ESTABLISH BOOKENDS

Talk to each of your departments (legal, HR, finance, operational) and gather a list of their 'hard stops': things that we just cannot do as a company for our customers, and why. Now take these to your team and, rather than just reading out a set of rules, ask them to create an imaginary scenario for each of these bookends, exploring how they might be broken and what the results might be. Bring a sense of humour and playfulness to the situation; you might even ask them to role play. Their final set of stories could even be turned into a video or booklet about 'what we are not'.

Then, share your stories. Again

Remember, this chapter is all about tone. Principles and bookends are great, but to set tone you really need to help your people recognise when something sounds right for your company. You want them to recognise a customer conversation or action as "just the sort of thing that we would do".

As we've already established, the best way to tune up people's ears is by using stories. Unlike simple statements or rules, stories create patterns in our brains, forming 'reference maps' we can pull up in the moment, compare with our present situation and use to guide us towards the right judgement. If there aren't any stories, people have no point of reference and will revert to process, like Sarah in my story above.

Again, it's all too easy to think that you've given permission without having really done it, because you haven't gone through the hard work of finding and sharing stories that capture the tone of your ideal customer experience. Stories are essential here because permission can't be turned into a process. It is a people-powered phenomenon.

 IRL: MYTHIC PIZZA

I've always loved a certain story I'd heard about Zappos: a story that epitomised their permission culture but almost sounded too good to be true. So, when I spoke to Hollie Delaney, I couldn't resist asking her: is that story about pizza a myth?

"The pizza story's true!" Hollie laughed back. "I think it was Tony [Hsieh, Zappos' founder-CEO] and Fred [Mossler, who oversees merchandising]. They were with a vendor and they got back to the hotel at like two or three in the morning and she really wanted pizza, and the hotel said they'd already closed the kitchen, so she was really bummed. So, Tony said call Zappos, just to see what they would do. So, she called Zappos and said 'Hey, I want a pizza', and the person she called at first said 'Oh okay, we're Zappos, you know we sell shoes?' And she said 'Yeah but I really want a pizza', so the rep said 'Okay, I'll find a place for a pizza', so he found somewhere that would be willing to deliver a pizza to her hotel."

Hollie went on to explain exactly how far their permission culture reached. "It's not about a call time," she insisted, "it's not about an upsell, it's not about any of that kind of stuff. It's about making a personal and emotional connection with the customer. And that can be by finding a cheaper item even though we might not sell it and sending them to that site. That could be just talking to somebody because they want to talk to somebody. That could be helping them order a pizza because they don't know where to order a pizza in their town."

Inspired, our team at Blue Sky decided to do a little 'pizza test' of our own. We called up various organisations and said: "Hi, I'm actually a customer of yours. I can't get internet connection - are you able to get online and order me a pizza?" The answers were hilarious; we got everything from the definitive "computer says no" right the way through to "happy to help", and everything in-between. Most poignant was the one where we could tell that he really wanted to step outside process and help, but we could almost feel the breath of his line manager on his neck down the phone. In our first round of doing this, only one organisation passed the test, which begs the question: what about you? Would your people pass the pizza test? Would you want them to? Would the story of what they did have been squashed or spread?

In a slight aside, I recently shared this story with a group of senior leaders and asked them who they thought the one organisation was that passed our pizza test. One of them shouted out "Dominos", which was brilliant, if inaccurate! Since I started sharing this story with clients, the pizza test has gone a bit viral and my inbox is filled with managers across the country sharing their own positive stories of people passing the pizza test. Obviously, I'm delighted, though I'm also slightly worried I might be increasing the call volumes of the world's best-for-service organisations on a daily basis – I hope I don't get found out!

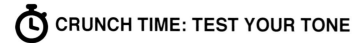 CRACK THE CODE: FIND YOUR PERMISSION STORIES

Launch a company-wide competition to collect stories about occasions when the people in your organisation absolutely nailed 'going above and beyond process for the customer' but in an appropriate and effective way.

These stories might involve conversations with and actions towards colleagues as well as customers, and could be captured in photos, videos, text or audio. One company I know designed a little book of permission stories called *50 Shades of Grey* - brave and brilliant! Or you might consider assembling them on one dedicated internal microsite and crowdfunding votes for the overall winner. As well as a prize, the winner would get to decide one new Symbolic Act the leadership team has to do every week, and this could become an ongoing initiative.

⏱ CRUNCH TIME: TEST YOUR TONE

I've designed these questions to really put the cat amongst the pigeons. So, take them to your front line teams and ask them to give their honest response. Then take them to your next Board meeting and ask the leaders of the company to fill them out. Then, right there in the boardroom (or is it an ivory tower after all...?), compare the two sets of answers.

1. Does your organisation know what it stands for?
A. Yes - we have absolute clarity and our culture is a living, breathing representation of that ethos
B. Almost - we have a clear and compelling ethos, but still a way to go to make it part of the DNA in everything we do
C. Not quite - it's hard to nail it to a mast, but there are good intentions in the way we operate today
D. No - words like ethos and purpose are up there with reaching out and socialise the idea on our organisation's bull***t bingo card

2. Do you have a set of agreed symbolic actions that leaders do to demonstrate commitment to people and customer?

A. Yes - I can cite at least three examples of Symbolic Acts in our organisation.
B. Sort of - there is good leadership intention in our organisation and leaders demonstrate commitment in their own ways, but nothing is formally known.
C. Ish - I can cite examples from lower levels of management, but examples would be thin for more senior levels of leadership.
D. No - the Ivory Tower is actually the name of the board room in my organisation.

3. Does your organisation have a permission culture?

A. Yes - we have a culture of full permission and we have stories in abundance to perpetuate the Artificial Intelligence engine of human judgement.
B. We're getting there - everyone here is empowered to do the right thing, but it is inconsistent .
C. We're working on it - we have some head in hands moments, but we understand the value of a permission culture and leader intention is good.
D. No - people should never be trusted with decisions. For all answers; see process. If process is absent, see Ivory Tower.

Do you still have a gap? If so, do not pass go, do not collect £200 - take your whole damn leadership team back to the start of the chapter. If you're getting all A's, however, you can polish up your little metal dog and roll the dice, because it's time to move on to Chapter 3 and spread your revolution to all the managers and team leaders in the business.

Yes, you're about to enter a new and balmy climate...

>_ SOURCE CODE: CHAPTER 2

- Tone is the first conversation that happens about who you are as a business, and it is set from the very top.
- To set the right tone, you need to be clear what you stand for. Create a strong ethos, then define tangible service principles that your front line teams can understand and act on to improve customer experience.
- To change the climate, you need to start by changing the stories, so turn your ethos into a compelling story – and share it again and again.
- 'Do as I say, not as I do' will not cut it. Undertake visible, consistent, repeatable and painful Symbolic Acts that demonstrate your commitment to what you stand for.
- Process only accounts for 80 per cent of what is required in a sales or service role; permission to do the right thing for the customer fills the gap. Establish bookends, share permission stories and dispel myths to model smart trust.

CHAPTER 3: CLIMATE CONTROL

BE MORE NOAH

When the bestselling author, marketing consultant and cultural anthropologist Simon Sinek visits Las Vegas, he likes to stay in the Four Seasons Hotel. I mean, who wouldn't? But Simon doesn't love the Four Seasons because of the fancy bed, the gourmet room service or the well-stocked minibar. Simon loves the Four Seasons because of Noah.

"I was in the lobby where they have a coffee bar one afternoon," he told me on a phone call we had. "I went to buy a cup of coffee and there was a barista there, by the name of Noah. And Noah was fantastic. He was funny, he was engaging, I was joking with him and chatting with him - you know I probably stood there for five minutes or longer, buying my cup of coffee. I think I gave him a 100 per cent tip.

"So, as is my nature, I said to him, 'Do you like your job here?' And without skipping a beat Noah said 'I love my job here.' So, I asked him, 'What is it, that the Four Seasons is doing, that you would say to me, I love my job?' Without skipping a beat Noah said 'Every day, managers will walk past me and will ask me how I'm doing and if there's anything that I need, to do my job better. Not just my manager, any manager.'

"And then he went on to say, 'I also work at Caesar's Palace and there, the managers are always trying to make sure we're doing everything right and will catch us if we do anything wrong. There I go to work, I put my head down - I stay under the radar and I just want to get to the end of the day and get my paycheck. When I come to the Four Seasons, I feel like I can be myself.'"

CLIMATE IS REAL

As Simon's story shows, the climate of an organisation isn't made up of the colour of its walls or the temperature the air conditioning is set to. It's composed of all the tiny things people say and do, from the moment they walk through the doors in the morning to the moment they head out for the night.

Climate can feel like the most 'intangible' of forces - a bit like weather. Just like the weather, it has a massive impact on your productivity and effectiveness (just think about how a dull, drizzly afternoon can drag down your energy and your to-do list). But if you look closely enough, you find that both climate and weather, as ubiquitous and chaotic as they might seem, are actually made up of thousands of tiny, concrete, scientifically observable events.

Conversations.

Yes, in the simplest terms, climate is the sum total of every conversation your organisation has, whether that's between customers and customers, customers and employees, employees and leaders, or within your front line and leadership teams. Really, this entire book is about climate, because your climate is the ultimate result of all that behaviour-training and mindset-shifting and uncoaching you're about to do.

But there are also seven distinct things that the best leaders do to kick-start and sustain climates where customer experience thrives, and that's what this chapter is about. Because although weather is a force of nature, climate is something you can control. And it is your responsibility, as leaders, to control it.

What's amazing is that so few leaders still take responsibility to control their own climate. There is now a good fifteen years of research[15] around the 'service-profit chain', which establishes the link between profitability, customer loyalty and employee satisfaction - in other words, the link between an organisation's climate and its financial success. Studies show that, when you're looking at the relationship between human capital and GDP, the single biggest differentiator in driving profit is the amount of 'discretionary energy', or willingness to contribute beyond the basic outlines of their work, an employee is prepared to expend,[16] and discretionary energy is a direct by-product of climate.

15 https://hbr.org/2008/07/putting-the-service-profit-chain-to-work
16 http://static.kornferry.com/media/sidebar_downloads/Korn-Ferry-Institute_Charged-up.pdf

However, here in Britain, we're still a bunch of climate-building amateurs. In a survey on employee engagement,[17] the UK ranked a sorry 19th out of 21 developed countries. There's that damn gap again.

The gap between what we know we need to do, and what we're actually doing. Why?

One reason is our old friend the tangibility bias. Leaders can be unwilling to invest in climate because, as we've seen above, they falsely consider it to be woolly and unmanageable. It's the organisational equivalent of Donald Trump denying the science of climate change because it is complex and requires money he'd rather spend on big shiny walls. Another issue is that leaders often misinterpret the need to control climate as the need to control people - what Noah might call the Caesar's Palace approach.

But if you ignore climate, an ineffective, disempowered and lacklustre customer experience will only continue to spread. If you try to force it to change, you'll get the same result. The only, and I mean the only, way you can create a customer-first climate is by helping your people to have better conversations. And to do that, you first need to make sure that every single exec, line manager, team leader and unofficial influencer in your company is personally demonstrating their commitment to your customer-first ethos.

Remember those 'tempered radicals'? It's time to mobilise a whole army of them. This is the point at which all leaders and managers - not just the ones at the top - must take responsibility for spreading the story of who you are and what you do, and role-modelling the kind of conversations they want to see show up on the front line.

Here are the seven ways leaders help their people get on board with their revolution.

---

17 ORC International Employee Engagement Index Rankings 2014

1. SPREAD YOUR WHY

Even in 2009, when Dan Pink published his bestselling book *Drive: The Surprising Truth about What Motivates Us*, he was drawing on decades of research. Frankly, it really shouldn't surprise anyone anymore when they hear that a sense of purpose matters more than a massive pay cheque when it comes to getting people to do good work.

But it does. It is still very hard for leaders to believe that a sense of purpose is *more* real than pounds and pence to the human brain, but overcoming this bias is essential if you are to get control of your climate. Purpose is the 'invisible electricity' that powers people at work - human WhyFi, if you will. The problem is, it only electrifies when it's *really* felt. There's a big difference between parroting a company's mission and truly internalising it. Can your people truly make the connection between the tough service conversation they're having at 3pm on a Wednesday, and your spirit-uplifting ethos?

As Pink puts it, "While complying can be an effective strategy for physical survival, it's a lousy one for personal fulfilment. Living a satisfying life requires more than simply meeting the demands of those in control. Yet in our offices and our classrooms we have way too much compliance and way too little engagement. The former might get you through the day, but only the latter will get you through the night."

Simon Sinek agrees that engaging with 'why' often comes from a sense of purpose under pressure, rather than a fake story that everything's great. "If you ask people what their best day at work was, nobody ever tells you about the day they got that big bonus or the day that they realised they made more money than they've ever made in their lives," he told me. "They talk about, you know, when everything went wrong and the whole team had to stay late and they all came together and it was an amazing night. Why aren't we telling those stories?"

Why indeed?

In the last chapter, we explored some powerful ways to share your compelling story. But there may well be something in your current climate that's blocking them from spreading and taking root in people's minds, and that something is likely to be negative beliefs.

Odds are, there's a decent amount of cynicism washing around in your company. You may have been through various 'transformation programmes' before, but without the right tools, skills or backing to make them stick. You may have produced several other stories in the past, without making the effort to bring them to life outside a PowerPoint. So, if you want to make this 'why' feel real, you'll have to work hard to shift and reframe (often perfectly justified) negative beliefs.

Listen out for the following beliefs, either spoken out loud or implied. "We've been here before." "This is never going to work." "Our leaders aren't committed to this." "This isn't going to make a difference to our customers." These are old beliefs that could be getting in the way of your new story. The people who hold them will be looking out for reasons to prove that they're right (a form of cognitive bias - something we'll explore more deeply in Chapter 5).

To shift these beliefs, you're going to have to get used to asking really smart questions that diminish the hold they have over people's minds, and reframe the way they think about their relationship with both your company and your customers. To do that, you're going to have to ask the ten questions below every time those catchphrases or ones like them show up.

1. Is what you're saying really true?
2. What evidence is there to support your view?
3. How does this way of thinking/view impact on the way you behave?
4. If you believed the opposite view, would it impact your behaviour positively?
5. What else could be happening?

6. What are the advantages/disadvantages of thinking this way?
7. Are you using 'extreme' language to support your thinking?
8. How much personal accountability are you taking?
9. What ideas do you have to change/influence the situation?
10. What is the benefit of focusing on things you cannot change?

These questions are based on the techniques from the field of psychology, so they're designed to press all the right 'transformation' buttons in people's brains. The first four are specifically attributed to the work of Byron Katie, an expert in the method of self inquiry.[18] However, when it comes to changing beliefs, slow, steady and consistent is the only way to win the race, so you'll need to work through them with yourself and your team again and again. That's right - it's broken record time.

Legend has it that JFK, while taking a tour of NASA, asked a janitor what he did for a living, and the janitor replied that he helped to put a man on the moon. That's purpose. That's it. That's what you're looking for.

 ## IRL: FIFO

I once worked for somebody who literally said to a group of people "Fit in or f*** off". To be honest, most leaders have had a FiFo moment or two; it can be incredibly frustrating when people seem to be resisting a story you've worked so hard to get right. But the angry toddler reaction will only entrench them in their existing mindset. So, don't be a Fifocker. Be a tempered radical, go undercover, and do the incremental work to engage people in your revolution.

---

18 Loving What Is: Four Questions That Can Change Your Life by Bryron Katie

LEADERSHIP HACKS: SPREAD YOUR WHY

i) Self-reflect

Consider yourself, do you have any limiting or negative beliefs? You may find yourself leaking your thoughts or verbalising negative feelings unintentionally. The thing is people will not believe, trust and follow a leader that does not believe in the change that is required. So, use the ten 'shift and reframe' questions to self-coach and change your own mindset.

Importantly, share your intent with your people; ask them to support you in challenging your own negative and limiting beliefs, calling you out when they see them and asking you how you are progressing in your own shifts.

ii) 1:1

Consider your team members, asking who has a limiting belief about themselves that is holding them back. Ask their permission to have a private conversation about this. Use our ten questions above to guide the discussion. But don't just use it as a script - make sure you are listening deeply and responding to what they say, not just asking the next question.

iii) Influence the influencers

Engage with informal leaders; these are the people that don't necessarily hold a leadership title, but are perceived by others as 'important'; maybe they are a top performer or someone who has been around for a long time. If they are chatting in the canteen and saying "I have seen it all before, this will never happen", it will damage the change effort and poison the well. If you can get them to shift and reframe first, they can be your best advocates.

iv) De-bugging

Myths will fill the void if you don't quash them. Create the wrong story and it can quickly become viral, break trust and take a long time to root out. "Did you hear that John said we can only spend 3 minutes on the phone or we will get in trouble?" It is a leader's role to dispel these bad stories, so get close to your people, find the myths and bust them. Engage with the informal leaders again to stop the spread.

Schedule a meeting a couple of months down the line to facilitate a debate, using the following questions:

- In the past, what beliefs were you holding about your role, the organisation and this team?
- How have they changed now?
- What have you learnt about beliefs?
- Do any of you still hold any negative beliefs that we need to address?

If so, use the limiting beliefs questions to myth bust! Introduce the team to the accountability ladder (explained in Chapter 6); get them to think about their thinking and how accountable they are being. The key thing is to focus people's minds on things that are within their influence. There is no point in worrying about stuff they can't impact or control. For the worriers in your teams, remind them that 90 per cent of the stuff we worry about never happens.

2. TAKE VISIBLE DEMONSTRABLE ACTION

Another good way to shift and reframe thinking is by using VDAs.

In Chapter 2, we established the importance of your leadership team taking Symbolic Acts to set the new tone for the organisation. Now it's time for everyone else to come on board. Whereas Symbolic Acts are 'cultural signatures' - big actions that leaders take that become talking points - Visible Demonstrable Actions are things that everyone can do, on a daily basis, to model and broaden that behaviour at all levels of the company.

And whereas Symbolic Acts are by their nature pretty flashy, VDAs can be miniscule.

What if you made the effort to hold meetings in regional offices rather than taking conference calls? How about giving one specific piece of positive feedback to three different people every day? Or even rolling up your sleeves and helping the cleaner rub a nasty stain out of the shared kitchen carpet? Anything that tells your story of commitment to respecting and serving people above everything else applies.

Watch yourself, though; it can be easy to smuggle negative beliefs into VDAs. Hassling people to stop customer conversations within 3 minutes so they can serve more people? That's not it. Telling people they're important and booking lots of 1:1s, then cancelling them because someone more important suddenly demands your time? That's not it either. Be rigorous with yourself and those around you. Remember, it's not just what you do, but the spirit in which you do it, that creates climate.

There's some interesting science that backs up the power of VDAs. In the 1980s, a neuroscience research project carried out at the University of Palma in Italy studied how specific actions were associated with specific neurons. Working with monkeys, the scientists discovered that certain neurons fired within the monkeys' brains when they mirrored the researchers' actions and behaviours. This work laid the foundation for the seminal paper 'The Mirror-Neuron System',[19] which showed a clear link between mirroring and learning: work that has been further evidenced and validated across multiple cultures.

The implications? We continually learn from each other, often without realising, and this starts at the earliest stages of our existence; new-born babies match gestures from just 42 seconds into their lives. So, if you aren't showing your people what matters, then how can you expect them to make it matter too? Monkey see, monkey do.

It's a little bit like the 'broken windows' theory in criminology[20], made famous by New York mayor Rudy Giuliani. Pay attention to fixing the details you can control, and over time the wider climate will change.

19 http://www.annualreviews.org/doi/abs/10.1146/annurev.neuro.27.070203.144230
20 https://www.theatlantic.com/magazine/archive/1982/03/broken-windows/304465/

IRL: GANDHI ON COMPLIANCE

One Friday late last year, and after help from a couple of lovely colleagues who are far more tech-savvy than me, I found myself - for the first time in my Blue Sky history - actually up to date on all our compliance tests. I dashed off an instant email to everyone in the business:

"Hello you lovely people,

I am writing, really, to show off. Strike whilst the iron is hot, so to speak. For the first time, I am actually UP TO DATE on all compliance tests. (Thanks somewhat to Laura and Jen who helped me first 'find desktop' and then George, who came all the way downstairs to help me click one button 'refresh' so I could check the system was keeping my scores). Gill almost passed out when she heard the news. Seriously, she still thinks it's not real.

There's a Gandhi story that goes something like this:

A mother took her son to Gandhi to see if he could encourage him to stop eating sugar. Gandhi heard the mother's plea and then asked her to leave and come back in 2 weeks. The woman left, rather bemused, and then returned with her son 2 weeks later with the same request. Gandhi addressed the child: "Boy, stop eating sugar, it is bad for you." The woman said thank you and then, as she was leaving, turned around and said, 'I'm curious to know why you couldn't have just said that 2 weeks ago.'

Gandhi replied, 'Madam, 2 weeks ago I was eating sugar myself'.

So – I know there are never enough hours in the day to do what we do, I really do. I also know that some of you don't even have the time to pee, never mind do a compliance test. I equally understand that prioritising something that has perceivably limited value to any of us is really hard.

But, to be really honest, I am getting really tired of dealing with noise around our non-compliance on this. Gill and I get an email every other day on the matter.

So, for me, and my sanity, please can we all give it a big push over the next couple of weeks? I know some of you will be raising an eyebrow at the email, some of you might even want to punch me in the face through your screen (I know. I would want to myself), but it would feel soooooooooo good to be the part of the division that is not on the naughty list. It literally took me 30 minutes IN TOTAL to do all five tests. I had it in my head this would be a whole afternoon job. Nope. 30 minutes.

I can send this email today; I may never be able to send it again. So let's do this thing."

Company-wide completion of compliance tests rocketed, and I learnt an important lesson: you can't effectively preach something you're not doing yourself.

CRACK THE CODE: VDAS

i) Leading by example
Think about a personal VDA you could start doing tomorrow that would let your team know you're committed to making changes.

- Consider your own behaviours and the environment. Be really honest with yourself. Is there anything you do that is out of alignment with the climate you want to build? What does not support our new way of being? How are you going to change it?
- Choose one thing to change first and implement it first thing when you get into the office (unless you're reading this at work - in which case, do it now!)
- See if anyone on your team notices or comments unprompted
- Ask for feedback – how has it impacted your team members? What would they like to see more of or less of from the leadership team or you as a person?

- Keep doing it
- Every week, go through this process again and add a new VDA to your list...

ii) Spread the VDAs

Now broaden this out to the managers in your organisation at all levels. Call a meeting and ask team leaders to consider what they are doing now that is out of alignment with your why.

- Identify VDAs that will demonstrate a commitment to the customer and send a clear message to people that things are changing
- Agree a plan to implement them, including how you will all tell people what you are doing and why
- Hold each other accountable as a management team by discussing the results at the next meeting, based on feedback from your team members
- Agree to have humility and willingness to admit mistakes. Nobody's perfect. When you make a bad choice, let those who are watching and learning from you know that you made a mistake and how you plan to correct it. By apologising, admitting your mistakes, and accepting accountability, you will be demonstrating an often overlooked part of being a role model

3. PROXIMITY IS EVERYTHING

In a now-famous 1989 study, Sidney Yoshida concluded that executive-level managers were only aware of 4 per cent of day-to-day problems that affected the quality of products or services that were being delivered to customers in a company, while their frontline employees knew 100 per cent. And recent research from Bain & Company shows that, while 80 per cent of CEOs believe they deliver an excellent customer experience, a mere 8 per cent of their customers agree[21].

---

21 http://bain.com/bainweb/pdfs/cms/hotTopics/closingdeliverygap.pdf

That's right: we've found another gaping gap in most organisations. This discrepancy between what leaders *think* is going on, and what their customers and staff *know* is going on, shows just how easy it is to get out of touch with the real nature of your climate.

But there's more. A study by TLF Research for technology firm eShare[22] in April 2017 revealed that four in ten employees cannot name a single member of their Board. Out of 1,000 UK employees polled, 18 per cent said their Board was barely visible, and more than half felt it was out of touch with day-to-day operations at their company. Some 31 per cent of respondents said that they do not know or understand their company's vision and values, and only 36 per cent could name their own CEO. What's more, the diversity of leaders did not match the diversity of the workforce. 37 per cent said that there was not a single woman on the Board at their organisation, while 58 per cent said there was no-one under the age of 40 and 55 per cent cited no ethnic diversity.

So there's a deeper rift here: a profound lack of accord between the team at the top and the people on the front line. When *they* are so demonstrably not like *us* - and barely even visible - any attempts to spread a revolution through the ranks, end at the boardroom door.

The good news is that there is an incredibly simple tool available to leaders that will help them bridge both of these related gaps. The bad news is that it requires your physical presence, rather than an email or a memo, and it cannot be outsourced.

Proximity is all about being close to the customer and to your people - literally. If you spend a lot of time in the same places as your employees and customers, listening to and talking to them, you won't just know what the real issues are, and the best ways to fix them - you'll spread the story that you're committed to people above all else, simply by being there.

Yes, it takes time. No, it isn't about instant problem-solving and you can't always measure the direct outcomes of an hour spent wandering in the call centre, kitchen or on the shop floor. But how close you are to your people will have a powerful impact on three crucial areas:

- your ability to assess the extent of the gap between your vision of what good looks like and the current customer experience
- your ability to influence that experience and make the right changes happen
- your people's perception of how important both they and the customer are to you

One week, a food retailer we worked with tested this out by putting a note up in their stores. The note told any customers who had a problem with their service that day to call a hotline. Unbeknownst to them, the hotline went straight through to the Board, who took it in turns to answer their calls. As soon as the retail teams realised where the calls were going, service improved. And the Board learned more in that one week than they had for years.

Another great example of proximity comes from Sir Terry Leahy, former CEO of Tesco, who is widely credited with turning Tesco from Britain's third-biggest supermarket into the world's fourth-biggest food retailer in just over a decade. Prior to stepping down in 2010, Sir Terry was a great fan of spending time talking to and observing customers. In fact, he reputedly spent up to 40 per cent of his time talking to customers and in store. That's almost half his working life! Proximity? That's it!

Other companies such as Zappos, First Direct and Amazon make everyone, at every level in the business, regularly deliver customer service as part of their job. But however you choose to show up, the message it sends is this: making customers feel amazing is a priority for everyone, CEO or intern, and everyone in this organisation makes the effort to experience the (sometimes tough) reality of what that means.

 **IRL: THE LONG WALK**

Sir Richard Branson is a dedicated practitioner of the management technique called 'The Walkabout', MBWA (managing by walking around) or 'The Long Walk', and he credits it for helping create the renowned customer experience at the heart of the Virgin brand.

"I like to think I practised it all my life," he explains in an interview with business website Inc.[23] "But I think in this day and age, it is very easy to be out and about and not stuck behind a desk. And you're going to learn so much more. I mean, if I'm on one of our airlines, I will make a point of getting out and talking to a lot of staff, talking to as many of the customers as possible, having a notebook in my back pocket, listening. And I think, one of the key attributes to a good leader is listening, making sure that you write down the feedback that you get. And very importantly, make sure you act on that feedback when you get back to base. An exceptional company is the one that gets all the little details right. And the people out on the front line, they know when things are not going right and they know when things need to be improved. And if you listen to them you can soon improve all those niggly things which turns an average company into an exceptional company."

'The Long Walk' technique has been around a long time, but it really works. Small changes can make big differences; making coffee on a different floor every day of the week or taking a new route back from the meeting room to your desk every time can force you out of the hamster wheel of habit and lead to unexpected encounters. For most of us, there are parts of the office we never go to, our 'dead zones' - maybe because they're dark or remote. Force yourself to make everywhere a 'live zone'. Imagine a GPS tracker map in your head and make sure that, over the week, you've coloured the whole area in neon lines.

23 http://www.inc.com/eric-schurenberg/sir-richard-branson-put-your-staff-first-customers-second-and-shareholders-third.html

⚡ CRACK THE CODE: PROXIMITY

i) Familiarity test

Before you even think about customers, a good place to start is to think about how close you are to your team, or those who you work most closely with. So:

1.   Get a pen and paper.
2.   Write down the names of the people in your team.
3.   Now try to add the following information for each one:
   - partner's name
   - children's names
   - date of birth
   - a hobby or outside interest.

How did you get on? Were you able to complete it for everyone in your team, or were there only a couple who you are friendlier with and know well? If you want your people to show up every day and give discretionary effort over and above their role, then you need to invest time in really getting to know them and understanding what makes them tick.

Now set this task for all managers to complete about their own teams.

ii) Just ask

How do you spend your time - are you close to the customer conversations? How often do you talk with and about customers? Do you even use the company's products and services? How well do you know your people and what motivates them? Be honest with yourself. Ask your team to give you direct feedback on how proximate they think you are. Be prepared for some hard truths. Don't ask the question if you are not prepared and committed to making the change. Encourage other leaders and managers to do the same.

iii) Up close and personal
Spend at least one hour every week with your team, listening and observing customer and team interactions (if you're feeling really brave, it's even better to actually deal with customers yourself).

- Set a diary reminder to ensure it happens.
- After each 'proximity session' reflect on what you've learnt and what action you will take based on this learning.
- Ensure your team know you're doing it to increase your understanding of their situation and the customer situations.
- Ensure you're listening and observing the team, being curious, not criticising.
- Build trust with your team.
- After a few weeks of doing these proximity sessions, ask your team for feedback. How does it make them feel?
- Now take action to remedy the 'niggles' you notice in the service experience - and feed back to the team what you have done about it.

iv) Go walkabout
Listen to people closest to the information. People out on the front line know when things are not going right and they know when things need to be improved. And if you listen to them, you can soon improve all those niggly things which turns an average company into an exceptional company. Working towards this will build more effective relationships in your team, and create a greater sense of shared purpose and a common understanding of what needs to be done to deliver more human experiences. So go on a 'long walk' of your own.

4. DEMONSTRATE PERMISSION

In Chapter 2, we set the tone for a permission culture, by establishing bookends and sharing stories. Now's the time to get that culture on its feet, and to initiate and encourage small acts of permission throughout the business.

Start consciously by publicly rewarding and recognising when people do the right thing, even (especially) when outside of process. Make sure you do this at least once a day. It may be hard at first, and you may have to single out very small and specific things (such as an unexpected comment you heard a front line person make), but once you get into the habit of noticing these things, you'll spot many more - and many more will start to crop up.

Resistance is inevitable. People at your organisation may well have gone through years of trying to do things differently, and been repeatedly smacked back down or, worse, are fearful of the consequences. Permission does not thrive in a climate of fear and where there is an absence of trust. It's like the old story about how flea circus owners train their charges by putting them in differently sized glass jars - supposedly, while fleas can naturally jump 100 times their own height, they will eventually learn only to jump as far as the lid, even when released from the jar.

Again, reiterate to managers and leaders that permission doesn't have to mean anarchy. Process is great. The art lies in combining it with the freedom to be human when process doesn't fit.

A good example here is Netflix's 126-slide culture manifesto on SlideShare, titled 'Freedom & Responsibility'.[24] This deck has become famous as an example of 'hands-off management' but, if you read it carefully, you'll see that the responsibility part is as important as the freedom. The holiday policy may say that Netflix's employees can take a break whenever they need to, but the implication is that they also work whenever they need to, even if that means before nine or beyond five. Similarly, the open expense policy includes an expectation that employees will "act in Netflix's best interest"... and I can guarantee they wouldn't be hands-off if someone suddenly filed a receipt for a few hundred quid at the races!

---

24 https://www.slideshare.net/reed2001/culture-1798664

Permission enables autonomy, and autonomy, like purpose, has been scientifically proven to be an incredibly powerful human motivator. It creates space for people to exercise their own judgement - and sends the message that you trust their judgement, too.

Think back to our case study of the washing machine call handler from Chapter 2. Sarah had been programmed, through all the historical situations that she had been in, to believe that following the process was the best thing to do - or indeed, that it was her only option. Perhaps she'd been told off in the past for piling too much work on an already overloaded delivery guy. Perhaps a friend of hers in an entirely different company had been fired for bending the rules. Perhaps she was falling behind her targets that month and didn't want to get into a potentially messy back-and-forth. Perhaps she was new, and simply didn't have the confidence to know she could make a different call.

Those thought processes - those bits of human decision-making data - are what you need to explore when you're coaching permission to your team. Get right inside Sarah's brain and discuss how it could have been different. What it would have taken to make her feel free to 'do a special' for the woman with the five kids and stinking gym kit? Again, there is no blame here. Just an opportunity to jump higher than an invisible lid.

Another example comes from a team I was recently working with. As I observed customer conversations, I found myself quickly racking up examples of processes that were shackling the front line teams from doing the right thing. In one conversation, one team member turned to the customer and said: "I cannot do that; unfortunately the quickest I can get it there is by next Wednesday." But it turned out that, due to errors, the customer had already been waiting for the product for two weeks. So even though the process stated it took five working days to get the product reordered and delivered, the process had already failed. Checking with the manager, I established this was one of the 10 per cent grey areas where the team member could have exercised judgement and sped up the process.

 IRL: GET OUT OF THEIR WAY

In a lecture for the RSA,[25] Dan Pink tells a story of an Australian software company called Atlassian, whose leadership team give their developers permission, once a quarter on a Thursday afternoon, to work on anything they want, however they want, with whoever they want, for twenty-four hours. The only rule (and here comes the responsibility bit) is that everyone must show their results to the company at the end of the twenty-four hours.

"It turns out that that one day of pure undiluted autonomy has led to a whole array of fixes for existing software, a whole array of ideas for new products that otherwise would never emerge," Pink says. "Now this is not an incentive; this is not the sort of thing that I would have done three years ago before I knew this research. I would have said 'You want people to be creative and innovative, give them a fricken innovation bonus! If you do something cool, I'll give you twenty-five hundred dollars!' They're not doing this at all. They're essentially saying, 'You probably want to do something interesting. Let me just get out of your way.' One day of autonomy produces things that had never emerged."

CRACK THE CODE: COACHING JUDGEMENT

As well as noticing, telling and sharing your positive stories, you can keep the permission culture alive through more focused conversations around judgement. One of the challenges that arises is leaders who get too hung up on outcomes and whether the outcome was 'right'. That's not going to help. The minute you coach anybody on whether what they did was right or wrong they'll never step outside of process ever again. The key is to move back up the thinking chain and have the conversation about the thought processes that got them to that decision, because that helps you to understand how they got to their judgement. That's where the conversation should be had. We call it coaching judgement, and here's how you do it.

---

25 https://www.youtube.com/watch?v=u6XAPnuFjJc

- Tomorrow, identify an action where someone in your team stepped outside process or could have stepped outside the process.
- Set the context that you are wanting to explore their thought process to help them for future situations.
- Explain that it is a random example and its correctness is irrelevant to the coaching session. It is the approach that you want to explore with them.
- Begin with an inform, e.g.
  - » "I notice that you discussed xx"
- Follow this with a question about their thought process, e.g.
  - » "What were you thinking at that point?"
  - » "What were you aiming to get to?"
- Then a question around outcome, e.g.
  - » "How appropriate was the outcome you achieved?"
- Then a question about decision, e.g.
  - » "What stopped you from doing x?"
  - » "What gave you the confidence to do x?"
- Finally a question about next time, e.g.
  - » "If anything, what would you do differently next time?"

5. CLEAR THE PATH

What does a manager or leader do on their first day on the job? They spend time with their people, because they're the ones who are delivering the work - but also because they haven't got anything else to do yet. On day two, however, they might produce their first report. On day three they might get asked to join a project team. On day four they might be locked into back-to-back meetings. By the end of the week, the manager who began by spending all their time with their people is now spending most of their time on stuff that has little or no direct impact on day-to-day customer experience.

So how can we get back to that first-day behaviour? What are you prepared to do to clear the path for your managers and create the time and space for customers to come first?

This isn't about elaborate process re-engineering. Most businesses nowadays have a function or department dedicated to 'continual improvement', but that's not what we're talking about here. The sort of path-clearing that leaders need to do is much simpler and more human than that. It's about freeing up *your* managers and teams to do the work they need to do for the customer, right now.

The biggest villain here is time.

From emails to reports to expenses to meetings, our own client diagnostics prove that, time after time, managers with good intentions get defeated by lack of, well, time. Try it yourself. Grab a pen and write down a list of things you'd like to be spending time on, versus all the things you're actually spending time on. If you're anything like me, this can be a pretty frustrating exercise.

Unfortunately, whatever all those productivity ebooks tell you, no-one can 'manage' time. It's *way* outside our reporting line. We can only use it in smart ways. So, your job is to identify all the time-wasting stuff that is getting between your people and the customer and eradicate it, so they can spend more time get on with their actual job. Doing stuff that adds real value to real people, in other words.

IRL: WILL IT MAKE THE BOAT GO FASTER

On 24th September 2000, the rower Ben Hunt-Davis MBE was sitting in a boat on the starting line of the Olympic Games. Like many organisations, the boat contained people who had little in common except for one thing: the fact that their job was to make that boat go fast. The commentators were pessimistic. The public was sceptical. Everyone expected them to do the same thing they had always done, and get the same result. No medal.

But this time, the team was desperate to win. They knew that they'd put in months and months of work, so that, on that day, in that boat, they could change the story. They'd got into the habit of asking themselves, every day, whether they were deciding to get on the rowing machine for another training session or asking if they should nip down the pub: Will this make the boat go faster? They'd recognised that behaviours of slagging each other off were not going to make the boat go faster. Instead, they had agreed to:

- Ask harder and harder questions
- Accept every piece of feedback they received from other team members
- Go with the best idea – no compromises
- Believe that 'Today is going to be a great day because I will make it a great day'
- Recognise that working harder was not their differentiator to other teams: it was instead about working better and continuous improvement over time
- Reflect and learn from every mistake - making the same mistake twice was not on
- Trust each other - that everyone would take responsibility to do their bit

Hunt-Davis has created an entire leadership coaching career and an award-winning book out of this 'will the boat go faster?' philosophy.[26] It's so relevant when you're trying to clear the path. Whenever you find yourself about to go into a meeting or open an email or jump on a conference call, ask yourself: 'Will this make the boat go faster?'

If the answer is no, get up from your desk instead, go and spend time with your team. Because the answer in that case is always: YES.

Start small and act now.

---

26 Will it Make the Boat Go Faster?: Olympic-winning Strategies for Everyday Success June 2011 by Harriet Beveridge (Author), Ben Hunt-Davis

LEADERSHIP HACKS: CLEAR THE PATH

Here are some ideas as a starter for 6
- Just sit beside your people for fifteen minutes on the floor.
- Ask everyone to turn off push notifications on their phones.
- Allocate a once-a-month admin day.
- Make meetings more efficient by starting at odd times such as 9.20, enforce time limits, walk as you talk

One of our clients, a large energy provider, used to spend a lot of time producing 196 reports. Only 6 of them were ever really used, so we helped their leaders go on a push to clear the path, and 190 were ditched. And if anyone tells you they just can't reduce their admin mountain any more, refer them to Thierry Breton, CEO of the French IT services firm Atos Origin, who last year announced his plan to make Atos a "zero-email" company. That's right. Zero. Email.

But those are just examples. Each company's white noise is different, so you'll need to do some listening first to figure out exactly what you need to clear to have the greatest effect.

And accountability is important here too. Although you'll need to take the lead in path-clearing, you'll also need to make sure that your managers take ownership to clear their own paths and those of their teams on a day-to-day basis, as more time-wasting activities crop up. The accountability ladder, which we look at in Chapter 6, will be an important tool to use to make sure that people don't just shift blame for their brambles: they pick up a hoe.

 # CRACK THE CODE: CLEAR THE PATH

i) Clearing together
Get your team together in a meeting (on the floor if necessary…).

- Ask them how things are going, in terms of putting people first.
- Ask them what barriers are getting in their way.

- Allow them to brainstorm all the possible barriers - put them on post-it notes and collect them up, grouping them together where they overlap and have themes.
- Use the accountability ladder (Chapter 6) to discuss each barrier, asking:
  » Is the barrier something we can influence or not?
  » As a team we can overcome this barrier by...
  » As a manager I will support you to overcome this barrier by...
  » We will pass this barrier on to the leadership team
  » We will SUMO this barrier ('Shut up and move on' because there is nothing that can be done. It is outside all our circles and influence. This is a great approach from motivational coach Paul McGee[27]).
- Ensure you stick to your commitments and proactively clear the path for your team.

ii) Question KPIs
Gather the management team. Review your KPIs through the lens of first your people and then your customer, and ask yourself "Are we really measuring the right things if we want to make our climate more human?"

iii) Job offer
Create a continuous improvement advocacy role in your team, and make their progress an agenda item at every management team meeting.

iv) Just ask
Ask for regular feedback from your teams on how clear their path to putting people first is.

---

27 http://www.thesumoguy.com/

6. CATCH PEOPLE DOING IT RIGHT

Let me take you back for a moment to our room with the 500 leaders from FTSE 100 companies (I'd better order them some coffee soon…) While I'm running my workshop, I'll put up a slide at some point showing a 'maths test' that looks like this:

$$1 \times 1 = 1$$
$$2 \times 2 = 4$$
$$3 \times 3 = 9$$
$$4 \times 4 = 15$$

Within seconds there'll be a murmur that goes through the room; a fidget, a palpable twitch. I'll ask "Why are you twitching?", and they'll say, "Because you got one wrong!" To which I'll reply: "Okay… but isn't anybody twitching to tell me I got three right?!" I call it the #149 test, and it provides a very simple but telling reflection on the default nature of human climates.

Organisations, particularly those in the UK, are suffering from an epidemic of negative critique. Not that it's our fault. 'Negativity bias' is in fact a well-documented psychological phenomenon, and many industries, from journalism to politics, exploit the fact that negative thoughts, emotions or events have a greater effect on one's psychological state and processes than their neutral or positive equivalents.

It's not our fault. It's an instinct, hard-wired into our DNA. We're experts at negative pattern recognition, thanks to an ancient part of the brain called the amygdala, otherwise known as the 'lizard brain'. From the early days of human evolution, this primitive set of neurons has been trained to look out for danger in every new situation, in case we might need to fight or flee, and this instinct is very hard to switch off. So, we create patterns of potential danger even when there aren't any there. It's a hard bit of conversation code to crack, but essential if we are to spread organisational harmony, rather than disillusion and fear.

Think about the last time you got a really nasty piece of feedback at work. Can you remember who said it, how they said it, where and when? Can you remember how you felt? Are you feeling that same feeling now? Now try to remember the last time someone said something positive about your work. Can you remember who said it, how they said it, where and when? Can you remember how you felt? Are you feeling that same feeling now?

Science tells us that most of us are likely to find the first, negative memory much easier to summon up than the positive one, and to find it much more emotionally powerful, even if it happened a while ago. That's all thanks to cortisol, the hormone activated when we are under stress. When cortisol is released, it causes our heart rate to rise, puts glucose into our muscles, heightens our senses and essentially shuts down our higher human functions. That made sense back in the day when we had to be prepared to sprint from a sabre-toothed tiger at any moment; it's less helpful in the workplace, where higher human functions are a definite bonus.

IRL: THE SELFIE CEO

The chief executive of one well-known delivery company tells a story I love about a transformation journey his company went on: a journey that was particularly focused on the power of positive critique.

This chief exec thought it was really important that, when their vans were out there on the streets, the brand was in safe hands. He wanted to encourage a workforce who really believed in the brand: who looked good, took care in their appearance, were proud of their work. So, every time he was out and about on the streets, whenever he saw a particularly sparkly white van with their logo on, he would take a selfie, email the photo of the clean van to the depot manager with a big 'WELL DONE!' and ask them to pass his feedback on to the driver.

I was sharing this story with a leader from a financial services organisation when he said "My God! For the past twenty years, I've been roaming the streets in exactly the same way, but looking for dirty cash machines and emailing the branch manager to let them know!"

As leaders, we have a choice in life about whether we're going to create a culture of positive critique or negative critique. Which approach do you think works better to nurture a climate where customer experience thrives? The one that catches people doing it right, or the one that points the finger at those getting it wrong?

I'll give you a clue: it's not the one headed up by the guy with the phone full of photos of grubby cash machines.

It's only once you start trying to offer positive feedback that you realise how deep our tendency to look on the dark side runs. People tend to home in on "What you didn't do" or "What wasn't supposed to be". Even employing the old 's**t sandwich' method (hiding a negative between two slices of praise) doesn't work - our brain simply picks out and feeds on the filling.

Thankfully, as any positive psychologist will tell you, with repeated exposure, you can train your brain to notice and replicate the good in any situation. That's what happens in best-for-service companies. Their leaders continually gather, record and share positive stories of when people stepped outside of process in an effective way or had a great customer conversation, using them to model the level of permission they want in their team.

This isn't about sweeping challenges under the carpet, or expecting everyone to go around giving each other high-fives (come on, if you're British, you can barely manage a high-five without falling over). That's not it. But it is about showing your teams how to default to the positive and building a bank of positive stories that exemplify your climate at its best - what I call a #149 climate, which is based on noticing great work rather than highlighting what's wrong.

🔒 LEADERSHIP HACKS: CATCH THEM DOING IT RIGHT

It can take some time to get into the habit of catching people doing it right. Encourage managers to take your lead and do this both in team contexts and in 1:1 coaching.

i) Seven pennies
I learned about this mechanism from an old boss. At the time, he knew staff were doing great things every day with customers – and that he'd miss those things if he was tied to his desk.

So, each workday morning, he would put seven pennies in his right front trouser pocket. For an hour, he'd tour around the office, looking for people doing things right. When he found one, he'd wait for the appropriate moment to pull them aside, praise what he saw, thank them, and move on. In two minutes, he validated their contribution and commitment. As he left, he'd take a penny from his right front pocket and move to his left front pocket.

He kept meandering through the office until he'd delivered at least seven bits of praise in that hour.

ii) Prizes for praises
Draw a grid on the flipchart, listing each team member's name with a blank space next to it. At the start of the shift brief the team that today is the Compliment Me challenge. That means that for every customer who compliments you and your service, you will score a point. The person with the most points at the end of the shift will win a small prize.

Explain that every time someone receives a compliment from a customer they should come up to the flipchart and mark it next to their name. When they mark up compliments, praise them and find out how they generated the compliment.

Ensure that you debrief at the end of the day or at the next huddle and ask: How did you generate compliments? What did you do and say to conclude the customer interaction?

iii) Building your positivity muscle
The more you catch people doing it right, the easier it becomes. Challenge yourself to suspend all cynical thoughts and critical comments for seven seconds. Not too hard, right? Now extend it to seven minutes, then... yes, seven hours. If you can go a whole day without being critical, it won't just help strengthen your positivity muscle, it will have a surprising viral effect. See how that day influences your relationships and the behaviour of others in your team. Then repeat.

7. CHANGE THE STORY

Google 'top leader attributes' and you'll find everyone from Harvard Business Review[28] to the Society for Industrial and Organizational Psychology (SIOP)[29] offering lists of the essential competencies a modern-day leader should display. A quick review suggests that strategic thinking, willingness to innovate and technology skills are the most lauded three strengths, perhaps with a good dose of ethics and vision thrown in.

Nowhere is there mention of storytelling.

And yet, as you've hopefully realised by this point (because I've been banging on about it like the good stuck record I am), storytelling is the single most effective mechanism for creating a climate for customer experience to thrive every day. Stories are basically super-charged conversations, which model what good looks like and sneak your positive, customer-first service principles into people's brains. Remember Noah? Noah used the story of his experience at the Four

---

28 https://hbr.org/2016/03/the-most-important-leadership-competencies-according-to-
    leaders-around-the-world?
29 http://www.siop.org/article_view.aspx?article=1195

Seasons to convey how its climate works to Simon Sinek. Simon used that story to explain how climate works, in general.

And I used a story to set the tone for this chapter. See? Stories are everything. So, if you want to change your climate, you have to change the stories. It really is as simple as that.

CRACK THE CODE: COLLECT STORIES

You've been collecting stories since Chapter 2. Now it's time to start getting really creative with how you deliver them and encourage others to join in. Play with the data. Create infographics and scoreboards. Record three-second podcasts on your phone. Roam the office, roping in team members for quick video interviews asking them to relate their most successful recent customer experience. If you're a retailer, roam the shop floor doing the same with customers, or if you're B2B, record a clip from your partners and suppliers. Try to have - whisper it - fun.

⏱ CRUNCH TIME: TEST YOUR CLIMATE

- Book an hour in your schedule to test your climate. Go on, you can do it, however little time you think you have. Clear the path.
- Spend that hour walking the length and breadth of your office (yep, The Long Walk) with your phone in your hand, recording stories. Some of them you might overhear. Some of them might be offered to you. Sometimes, you might have to ask: "Tell me a story about what's going on at our company" or "Tell me a story about your work."
- At the end of the day, listen back to those stories. Summarise the 'message' of each one in a single sentence ('Customers are really angry at us'; 'Everyone here is tired') and give a positivity score from 0 (I hate it here) to 10 (I adore my work).
- Now add up all the scores and divide them by the number of stories to get your average score.

- If your score is below 5, you need to get your leadership team together, make sure you've really worked through the exercises in this chapter, and come up with a game plan. If it's between 5 and 7, keep going, but redouble your efforts. If it's 7 or above, throw your whole team an impromptu party with cake and beer - you're getting there!

Then redouble your efforts regardless, and move on to Chapter 4, where your climate is going to start blooming with new behaviours...

>_ SOURCE CODE: CHAPTER 3

Climate is the sum total of every conversation in your organisation, whether that is between customers or employees. It can feel intangible but it is something you can control, and it is your responsibility as a leader to control it.

To create the right climate and mobilise your tempered radicals, there are seven distinct things leaders can do:

1. Spread your why: purpose is the 'invisible electricity' that powers people at work, so become a meaning maker, dispel myths and help to reframe people's thinking.
2. VDAs: Visible Demonstrable Actions are things everyone can do on a daily basis to role-model the behaviours that will result in the right climate.
3. Proximity is everything: being close to your people and customer conversations ensures you are in touch with reality and know where there are gaps.
4. Demonstrate permission: this is not about anarchy but accountable freedom. Help people to make the best decisions for the customer, while balancing business needs.
5. Clear the path: our days quickly fill with white noise that does not make the boat go faster. Great leaders free up their people to focus on work that reaches the customer.
6. Catch people doing things right: there is an epidemic of negative critique stressing our workforces. The power of praise is what really helps drive climate change.
7. Change the stories: storytelling is the single most effective way of creating a climate where customer experience thrives. Think Noah: great stories travel like wildfire.

CHAPTER 4: NICE IS NOT ENOUGH

THE BIG EASY

In 2012, British Telecom was in trouble. In an interview with MyCustomer.com,[30] the telco giant's MD Warren Buckley admitted that, thanks to a restructure the company had implemented to separate the B2B and B2C service divisions, "We went through a nine-month period where we let down many customers, our reputation dropped and we responded by putting in a lot more staff who weren't well enough trained. So, we responded to a crisis and, in some ways, we then made that crisis worse."

What followed was a thorough overhaul of sales and service processes and behaviours, a project that didn't just dig BT out of its customer experience hole, but which transformed the company's understanding of what its customers really want.

Deciding to enhance their Net Promoter Score (NPS) and Customer Satisfaction (CSAT) scores, BT measured every single customer experience that occurred across every channel in the company, by asking "Overall, how easy was it to get the help you wanted from British Telecom today?"

This huge research project revealed that customer effort was the number one driver of advocacy amongst BT's customers, above brand warmth, reaction to billing, value for money and reliability. When the company experimented, varying its technology and tactics then re-evaluating how each tweak affected the 'ease' of the experience, it concluded that, when it came to 'making the boat go faster' for its consumers right now, a seamless, multichannel approach was the holy grail.

"We respect the channel that the customer chooses," Buckley reported. "We measure the easiness of each of those channels, but we will promote certain channels if we think they're better, not just for us but for the customer as well [...]

---

30 http://www.mycustomer.com/service/channels/warren-buckley-bt-how-measuring-customer-effort-saved-our-service-operations

"The key for us is you've got to connect all those together. Where the service industry is now is we've gone from single channel to multiple channel: the next step is to go to multichannel. To actually make sure that the customer can start on their smartphone, then use their laptop, then call us, then tweet us, and that we know that journey."

BT had discovered that delighting their customers was less important than making things easy for them. So, the question you need to ask yourself now is: what's your customer experience sweet spot?

THE NEW BRILLIANT

As we saw in Chapter 2, the consensus as to what a good customer experience looks like has changed a lot over the decades. This shouldn't be surprising - what we expect from brands, and how we interact with them, is directly connected to our economy, society and technology, all of which are currently changing at a lightning-fast rate.

In a digital economy, polite and professional is no longer good enough. We're time-poor, one-click, cross-channel, relentlessly social creatures. We expect all our data to be auto-filled. We conduct extensive market research with a quick Twitter poll. We buy now, opt for same-day delivery, and move on. Of course, warmth and friendliness are still important, but they're no longer the behaviours that are going to inspire customer love and loyalty.

There have been plenty more case studies to back up the importance of a low-effort experience since. Yet the vast majority of service and sales departments still put a premium on 'soft skills' such as empathy, and they still use analytics built to measure and reward behaviours that simply don't cut it anymore.

When you look at the induction content today for large companies, it hasn't evolved much further than the 'smile when you dial' mantra from the late 1970s. But does smiling when you're dialling drive up customer satisfaction?

We wanted to find out, so we combined analysis from 1,080 conversations, across seven different sectors in 17 FTSE 100 companies. The result? There is no significant difference in the politeness of the staff between conversations where customers were very satisfied or very dissatisfied.

In a similar vein, we've seen training materials that suggest service staff should profusely apologise and demonstrate 'six stages of regret' when dealing with a customer issue. One FTSE 100 firm even used their new speech analytics machine to measure how frequently their people were apologising. They then created league tables and made this one of the key performance indicators (KPIs). But surely you know your training isn't working when you hear "I'm so sorry for your loss regarding those mouldy strawberries" - let alone know that such nonsense is being rewarded!

The same FTSE 100 firm also insisted that at the end of every conversation, its people would ask "Is there anything else I can help you with?" Yet when we reviewed the data from over 3,229 customer calls, this strategy had no correlation at all with the level of customer satisfaction.

Most organisations know they need to upgrade their conversation code, so they're trying out various so-called 'best practice' strategies to improve their results. Unfortunately, although they differ from place to place, these strategies tend to have one thing in common: they most definitely don't come from a detailed analysis of the behaviours that the company's top performers demonstrate. Instead, they most likely arise out of a well-intentioned belief from someone in L&D that these nice-sounding behaviours 'should' make a difference.

Oh look: could that be another gap cracking open beneath our feet? Because it's one thing to realise that your old behaviours aren't working anymore - but it's quite another to be able to identify and put into place the ones that will actually move the customer experience dial for your business.

Welcome to Chapter 4.

Here at Blue Sky, we've spent years analysing tens of thousands of sales and service conversations from dozens of companies, from telcos to water to retail to banking. Determined to let go of any old assumptions and biases, we've interrogated the resulting data with fresh eyes and looked at it through the lens of the latest scientific thinking in an attempt to redefine the behaviours that drive a brilliant customer experience, right now.

What we discovered was four common truths: four behaviours which turn out to be effective for any organisation that wants to drive a high service experience today.

There is a qualification to be made here. Inevitably, certain behaviours are more effective for certain organisations, certain behaviours are more effective for certain customers, and some will come more easily than others to your teams. The fact is it's up to you to investigate and identify your company's number one sweet spot. But our findings are clear: all of these four behaviours, whatever your sector, will help improve your customer experience in a real, measurable way. What's more, each one of them is backed up by science-derived 'brain bytes' - fresh insights gleaned from fields such as psychology, neuroscience and behavioural economics that show how we can engineer customer conversations for an optimal outcome.

It's time to get down to the nitty gritty of making this work on the front line. Let's go.

BEHAVIOUR 1: ADVOCATING

In its simplest terms, advocating means demonstrating to a customer that you're on their side.

The truth is that most customer conversations take place because something has gone wrong. A product has broken, a service has failed, someone is disappointed, inconvenienced, annoyed. Much of good service boils down to how a company reacts in those scenarios; how effectively you can turn around a situation that starts off on a negative note.

Conventional service wisdom tells us that this is the moment to use empathy. But the dictionary definition of empathy is the ability to understand and share the feelings of others and if you're talking to fifty or even a hundred het-up customers every day, that's a hell of a lot of feelings to understand and share. Empathy is hard enough to achieve in a single conversation with your partner; it's impossible to achieve with a hundred strangers a day.

What you end up with is 'false empathy' instead. We've all been on the receiving end of statements like "I understand how you feel", "I'm sorry to hear that", dutifully rolled out over the phone without any emotional truth. And far from improving the situation, these sorts of statements often make it worse. We don't want our gas company to give us a hug; we want them to sort out our pipes.

This is where advocating comes in. Advocating is a behaviour specifically designed to make the most of that first magic minute of a customer conversation (see the science behind this in the Brain Bytes bit). It achieves the intended result of false empathy without any of the downsides, giving the customer an immediate sense that they are safe in your hands.

Advocating for the customer has three stages:

1. Genuinely acknowledging what has been said (without false empathy).
2. Accepting accountability (without excuses or blame).
3. Explaining what action you're going to take to solve it (now).

So what does advocating look like in practice?

When something has gone wrong, you might say: "Well that doesn't sound right at all but you're through to me now, so let's see what we can do."

For a discrepancy on a bill, you might say: "That sounds as though we've confused you a bit there. You're through to the right place. Let's see if I can explain what's happened and then we'll sort it out for you."

When I tell people about advocating, they often ask if I'm suggesting that they shouldn't say sorry anymore. The answer to that is a resounding no! As a human being representing the company you work for, when a human being tells you that something's gone wrong, it's absolutely right to apologise. But you do need to follow it up with a sentence that inspires confidence in your ability to do something about it.

That's why advocating really works. It's the double whammy - I agree with you, and I'm in control of what happens next - that creates rapport and establishes trust. All our evidence shows that this has a significant impact on the success of the first sixty seconds of the conversation. And what happens in the first sixty seconds determines the way the whole customer experience will unfold.

🧠 BRAIN BYTES: THE MAGIC MINUTE

We're all familiar with the old chestnuts that 'first impressions count' and 'first impressions last'. Well, as is often the case, there's some fascinating scientific truth behind these two nuggets of folk wisdom.

The first comes from the psychological technique of 'thin slicing'. Psychologists have done research to determine whether people can predict the outcome of a conversation based on listening to its first few seconds.[31] They discovered that we can, and do, with an impressive degree of success. This ability, called 'thin slicing', is a central part of what it means to be human, as we've been conditioned over thousands of years to unconsciously and accurately judge others very quickly. So even now, whenever we meet a new person, or need to make sense of a new situation quickly, we automatically 'thin slice'.

Our takeaway? In a customer conversation, it's crucial to nail the first sixty seconds if you want the rest to be perceived as a success.

This is backed up by research we've done here at Blue Sky. We listened to the first minute of a significant sample of conversations, and correlated the customer's satisfaction score for the first minute to their rating for the whole experience. Our findings were clear: a customer's first impressions overwhelmingly set the tone for their whole experience. The first 10 per cent of the conversation dictates the way the next 90 percent goes, because that first 10 per cent is 100 per cent of a customer's experience, at that moment. As the conversation goes on, the intensity of the experience gets diluted; the second minute is only 50 per cent of their experience, the third is 33 per cent, and so on. The front-loaded intensity of a customer's experience is another reason we call the first sixty seconds of conversation the 'magic minute'.

---

31 Ambady, Nalini; Rosenthal, Robert (March 1992). "Thin slices of expressive behavior as predictors of interpersonal consequences: A meta-analysis". Psychological Bulletin. 111 (2): 256–274.

There's a second pearl of knowledge that adds to this insight around the magic minute, and it concerns the snap judgements we make when we meet new people. In her book *Presence*, Harvard psychologist Amy Cuddy[32] reports that people instinctively ask two questions in their head when they meet someone new. The first is: 'Can I trust this person?' and the second is: 'Can I respect this person?' (otherwise known as the criteria of 'warmth' and 'competence', respectively). Interestingly, most people, especially in a work environment, think competence is the more important quality. In fact, our level of warmth has a far greater influence on how we are judged. This makes evolutionary sense; in Neolithic times, it was less important to know that your new friend was good with an axe than to feel confident that they wouldn't stab you in the back with it. Competence is important, of course, but it's only evaluated once we've established trust.

Our takeaway? In those crucial first sixty seconds of a customer conversation, your absolutely priority has to be establishing trust. And advocating is the best way to do it.

⚡ CRACK THE CODE: ADVOCATING

i) Nightmare scenarios
Get your team together and identify your top 'nightmare scenarios': things that could go horribly wrong on a variety of customer conversations. Then work together to identify a number of ways that you could respond to each one that:
- demonstrate they are on the customer's side
- reassure them that they will sort it out for them.

Then ask them to consciously practise advocating for the customer in their next conversation and see the impact it has. Get back together to share positive stories of the most effective strategies. You could even compile them into a best practice advocating toolkit.

---

32 Presence: Bringing Your Boldest Self to Your Biggest Challenges Jan 2016 by Amy Cuddy

ii) Rewrite
Print off ten customer letters, emails and transcribed webchats. Ask your team to review them through the eyes of advocating. Score them, with 1 being 'miles away' and 10 being 'on the money'. Where there is opportunity for improvement, get the team to use advocating to rewrite the printouts until they achieve a higher score.

iii) Leading by example
Explain to your team that, this week, you are going to focus on advocating for the customer. Before the session, go on the phone or shop floor yourself and demonstrate advocating for the customer well. Ensure that you really demonstrate best practice - showing the customer you are on their side and are going to take action to help them: i.e. "Jenny, that is simply not good enough and not the sort of service I would want you to have. You're through to me now and I will sort this very quickly. To do that I will ask you a few questions, is that OK?"

Record the calls or get the team to observe you having the conversations. Ask your team to discuss what was good about them and how you demonstrated advocating.

iv) Fresh starts
Encourage your people to do these things:

- Listen to or observe five customer conversations, looking through the lens of 'Am I creating a great first impression?'
- Practise different openings to the conversations that sound warm and positive.
- Practise using acknowledging statements with customers, ensuring that you are demonstrating to them you are listening i.e. "In summary, you are looking for X and Y, I can certainly sort that out for you. To do that, I'll run through a few questions to find out a bit more, if that works for you?"

v) Engage imagination
Ask your team for things customers typically say, which would require

the skill of advocating i.e. "Someone promised to call me back, and they never did" or "I've been passed from pillar to post by you lot!"
Flip chart their responses, and ask the team to come up with ways that would demonstrate advocating in reply.

vi) Accountable advocacy
In pairs, ask your team to discuss how they could demonstrate more advocating and the impact it would have. Ask each team member to commit to demonstrating more advocating this week, and log one conversation on the flipchart (time/date/name) where they demonstrated great advocating.

Use it as a basis for the next 1:1 coaching conversation you have with the team member, celebrating their success, discussing what went well, the impact and the opportunity they have to do more of that.

vii) Pledges
Ask each team member to pledge one small change they will focus on today, linked to the magic minute, which will make a big difference to their performance, how they feel or how the customer responds to them. Record these on the flipchart and revisit them during the day to find out how they are going.

Celebrate each small change, big difference at the end of the shift and debrief by asking:

- How did it affect you?
- How did it affect your customers?
- How did it affect your results?

viii) Advertising change
One of the ways to support yourself when you're learning new things and making changes is to 'advertise your change'. Talk to your team about the fact that they've probably tried to make a change before, and it hasn't happened. Why is that? One reason people fall at the first hurdle is because they don't tell anyone about the changes they intend to make.

So, get your team to tell colleagues and line managers of the changes they intend to make - and not just tell them, but ask for their help and feedback too. By actively advertising their change and asking for the support and help of others, they're much more likely to make a change that sticks.

And do the same yourself! Remember: you need to lead by example. So, advertise the changes you're planning to make yourself to colleagues in the leadership team.

BEHAVIOUR 2: USING EFFORTLESS LANGUAGE

We've already established that, for a time-poor generation brought up in an instantly-gratifying world of apps and algorithms, the best service feels easy. But we also know that good service and sales require a great deal of effort - practical, technical, emotional.

So how do we close that gap?

With language. Climate is built from conversations, and conversations are built from language, so mastery of language is the ultimate service skill. However, all too often we let our language control us, rather than consciously choosing the words that will deliver us the best possible result.

As customers, we've all experienced the 'computer says no' moment, when human sales and service people talk to us like pre-programmed robots, designed to block our desires at every turn. In these conversations, language becomes a barrier, and our words clash against each other until we reach a stalemate. It's the opposite of effortless.

By contrast, effortless language has three characteristics. It is:

- positive
- accountable
- easy

Using positive language doesn't mean exclaiming 'awesome' every five seconds. "Wow! Brilliant!" That's not it. Positive language is all about intent. It means noticing and praising good choices and successful moments in the conversation: not just using positive words, but signalling your positive intent to the customer, your determination to be on their side.

"That sounds great, Mr Smith, really good choice."

Similarly, accountable language doesn't mean adopting a defensive tone, or insisting that "I'm doing everything I can for you here, Mr Smith!" That's not it. Accountable language means giving the customer absolute trust that they're safe in your hands.

"You've got me now. You're through to the right person now. Let's sort this out."

Finally, easy language doesn't mean struggling to make things clear by walking the customer through every step in the process: "Well, first you open your browser, then you go to our website, then you go to the menu, then you navigate to this page, then you look on the top right-hand side for the link to download this form, then you…" That's not it. Easy language means making things feel as simple as possible, and offering to give more detail if required.

"I'll just send you the link, then you download it, fill in the form and send it back to us. I can walk you through that if that would help." That's it.

 BRAIN BYTES: LABOUR INCLUSION

In a customer conversation, there's usually an awful lot going on above and beyond the words. Information needs to be looked up, data needs to be keyed into the relevant fields on the screen, systems need to be navigated, notes need to be logged… all while trying to advocate and use effortless language and maintain an all-round engaging experience.

Sales and service people need to do this stuff to be helpful but, all the time they're busy working away, the customer is listening to silence, and oblivious to what is happening on the other end of the line. But surely, you might think, this is part and parcel of getting service right? Surely customers interpret our busy silence as a good thing?

Unfortunately not. Some new and interesting data tells us that if we can keep the customer involved in what we're doing, it can have a significant impact on their experience. This comes from website research around booking flights that demonstrated a difference in customer experience depending on what was happening on the screen. Some customers were shown a buffering circle turning in the centre of the screen while flights were being searched for. Other customers were given information on what was actually happening ('searching 200 hotels… 300 hotels… checking flights…'). In other words, the second set of customers were being included in the labour that was taking place in the background.[33]

The technical term for this is 'labour inclusion' - when someone describes exactly what they are doing when carrying out a job or action - and the research found that the customers who were kept engaged using labour inclusion rated the website, and their experience, significantly better than those simply shown the buffering symbol. Interestingly, they also perceived the wait time to be a lot shorter, even though it was exactly the same in both tests. Conventional wisdom suggests that the longer people have to wait, the less satisfied they become. Instead, it turns out that when the customer is included and given a sense of the work being done for them, they don't just not mind the wait - they value the service more.

So labour inclusion should be a part of every customer conversation. Telling the customer what you're doing, why you're doing it and keeping them in the loop while you're doing it will greatly enhance their engagement in the conversation and reduce their feeling of effort.

---

33 Based on the work of Ryan Buell and Michael Norton from Harvard who coined the term "labor illusion"https://hbr.org/2011/05/think-customers-hate-waiting-not-so-fast

CRACK THE CODE: EFFORTLESS LANGUAGE

i) Mind your language
Ask your team to choose one of the stock statements they use on a daily basis around a process or product (whatever is relevant to them).

- Get them to speak it out loud to an imaginary customer, all the time transcribing it on paper.
- Then get them to examine the language they use, checking and rewriting every sentence and word for maximum positivity, accountability and ease.
- Now ask them to take it back into their customer conversations and monitor the difference it makes.
- Feedback as a group about the most useful words and phrases they found.

ii) Positively charged
Ask the team to think about their last five written customer correspondences and answer the following questions:

- What negative news did I have to give to my customer?
- How could I have positioned this news more positively?
- What language did I use?
- What language could I have used to transform the correspondence?
- What will I say next time I have to give this news so I position it more positively?

iii) Effortlessly brave
It's time for your team to be really brave. Ask them to pick five colleagues who they work closely with. These could be fellow team members, line managers or internal customers. Get them to ask:

- What do I do well that makes it easy and effortless for my customers (or 'for you' if you have internal customers)?
- What could I be doing that would make it easier and more effortless for my customers (or 'for you' if you're asking internal customers)?

When they have their feedback, ask them:

- What will you do more of?
- What will you do less of?
- What will you start doing?

Encourage them to go public with the changes they're going to make, and to share their feedback at their next 1:1.

iv) Strong signposting
Encourage your team to do these things:

- Listen to or reflect on five conversations, looking out for areas where there are long silences or the customer has not been informed of what is going on.
- Practise signposting at key stages of the customer conversation or written correspondence: "What I am now going to do for you is…" or "Thank you for that information. To sort that out for you I'm going to ask you a few questions so I can really understand what's going on."
- Ask permission and gain buy-in, using 'Is it ok if I…' type questions.
- Use clear and easy-to-understand language, avoid baffling customers with jargon and techy speak.
- Make it positive – use outcome-focused language "This will enable you to…"

Then discuss with your team: how did they handle long silences? What types of signpost did they use during the conversation? How did customers respond?

v) Backwards bingo
Write up on the flipchart five negative phrases that you know your people use in their customer conversations. You'll be able to make these really specific to your business area. Some examples might be:

- "I'm afraid that is not possible"
- "I appreciate what you're saying, but…"
- "No, we can't do that here…"
- "You will have to phone another number for that…"
- "That is not our policy…"
- "What you will have to do is…"

Ask the team to think of ways to rephrase these so they demonstrate effortless language. Now place these effortless language phrases on a bingo grid. The team will have to get these phrases into their customer conversations during the day and each time they do, they can cross them off the bingo grid.

Tell the team that if these phases are used in their customer conversations today, you'll personally go on the phone/ floor / answer emails/letters/webchats for one hour per bingo line (and then follow through!)

vi) Teach back
In morning team meetings, ask a colleague to 'teach back' what labour inclusion is and is not. They have 90 seconds to explain the brain byte. Then play this YouTube video of an internet buffering wheel *http://bit.ly/BlueSkyBuffering* and link the concept back to customer conversations.

Discuss how does it feel to be kept waiting when you don't know what the service person is doing or why? How can we include our customers more so they know what we are doing and why?

BEHAVIOUR 3: FLEXING

You should always 'treat others as you would like to be treated yourself, right?

Wrong! Not if you want to create amazing customer conversations. It's only when you treat others as *they* would like to be treated that you can deliver the best possible customer experience.

The thing is human beings are not blank slates; we come to each encounter preloaded with a cluster of historic preferences that determine how we behave. When these preferences meet with someone else's in conversation, sometimes they blend - and sometimes they collide.

It's so important to be able to communicate with our customers in a way that suits them. If a customer says: 'This happened at two o'clock on Thursday, and this had just taken place, and this was going on in the background', you'd better bet that they're a detail person, who'll want lots of specifics. But if the sales or service person is a big picture person, determined to skim over the small stuff to get to a resolution, their communication is doomed to fail.

That's where flexing comes in. Flexing allows us to adapt our language and behaviour to best fit the individual we're talking to. Flexing asks that we first understand what our own default behaviours are; then, once we understand ourselves, we can identify how we need to adapt our own behaviours to chime with those of the customer, for optimal results.

And as we've seen, it's important to hit the right note from the start. But it's obviously also impossible to provide a perfectly bespoke experience for someone you first met a second ago. For this reason, we've developed four simple behaviour types, so we can quickly identify the 'kind' of person a customer is and the behaviours that they are likely to respond to best.

Now, sometimes people get anxious when they hear about these types. They've come across elaborate profiling tools before, and they worry that they won't be able to 'get it right'. Fortunately, in this case, it doesn't matter. You don't need to be a psychologist to flex. Once you've familiarised yourself with the types - and I can guarantee you'll have friends, family or colleagues who fit into each one - you don't even have to remember them. Just start picking up on the conversational cues of the customer you're talking to - i.e. listening - and it will instantly become obvious which behaviours they prefer.

The four types are:

1. The Loyal Connector: an empathic, caring 'people person'
2. The Competitive Driver: a quick, targeted decision-maker
3. The Logical Analyser: an organised, lover of detail
4. The Creative Enthusiast: a positive, energised brainstormer

The best way to understand these types is to imagine them in real-life scenarios. So picture this: you're out for the night at a crowded bar with your mates (a distant dream for most mothers of three!) If you're a Loyal Connector, you'll give way to the people around you, murmuring "Excuse me, you go first". If you're a Competitive Driver, you'll barge past the Loyal Connector and slam your £10 note down on the bar. If you're a Logical Analyser, you'll stand back and figure out which part of the bar is moving quickest, and which bartender is most efficient, then target them. Or, if you're a Creative Enthusiast like me, you'll chat to everyone around you, then when you finally get to the bar you'll dither for ages before crying "Sod it - I'm on a night out - I'll have a bottle of champagne!" (And then when you get back home, your Logical Analyser partner will respond: "And how much did you spend on that?!")

Or imagine you're packing a suitcase for a two-week summer holiday. A Loyal Connector will pack weeks in advance and ensure they have covered every eventuality for every member of the family, from diarrhoea tablets to kids' colouring books, leaving hardly any space for their own clothes. A Competitive Driver will either delegate the whole exercise or pack in one quick, efficient burst, following a short bullet-point list. The Logical Analyser will painstakingly pack the most perfect suitcase akin to a game of Tetris, with bags for dirty clothes and allocated room for in-trip purchases. The Creative Enthusiast, on the other hand, will shove a last-minute armful of random glad rags into a bag, and celebrate the chance to go shopping for everything they inevitably forgot (ahem).

Which one do you feel closest to? Which one has the greatest chance of getting your back up? Which one describes your boss, your colleague, your partner, your best mate?

In an ideal world, we should all be flexing, all of the time. It's an amazing behaviour to master in your personal life; it really does allow you to make friends and influence people. For effective customer experience, it's absolutely essential. Plus, the more you do it, the easier it gets.

LEADERSHIP HACKS: FIND YOUR FLEX

If you're going to teach FLEX to your team, you'd better start by knowing your own type. So, we've devised a short test to diagnose which of the four types fits you best. You can then take it to your teams and walk them through it too. Go to the appendix for the full set of FLEX questions and get to know yourself now!

BRAIN BYTES: COGNITIVE BIAS

Do you believe that you possess above average intelligence? Do you believe that the vast majority of people are honest? Reflecting on your day, can you remember more things that went wrong, than right? Do you think that the best-performing member of your team is the one who got the highest score in their latest review? Do you tell yourself you're not going to drink in the week, then cave on Monday night?

If your answer to any of the above statements is yes, you're suffering from cognitive bias. In its eagerness to turn the world into a manageable, ordered place, the human brain is programmed to serve up versions of reality that aren't, well, real. The concept was first defined by the psychologists Amos Tversky and Daniel Kahneman in 1972,[34] and everyone from governments to sports coaches now use its insights to make better decisions and influence others more powerfully.

In order, the statements above are examples of:

- Self-enhancement bias (80 per cent of us see ourselves as above average which is, obviously, impossible)

34 Kahneman, Daniel; Shane Frederick (2002). "Representativeness Revisited: Attribute Substitution in Intuitive Judgment". In Thomas Gilovich; Dale Griffin; Daniel Kahneman. Heuristics and Biases: The Psychology of Intuitive Judgment. Cambridge: Cambridge University Press. pp. 51–52

- Confirmation bias (we seek out people and information that matches our beliefs - if you believe people are honest that's what you'll look for if not, you won't)
- Negative bias (remember 'Catch people doing it right' from Chapter 3?)
- Recency bias (a recent experience can have a more powerful effect on our decision-making process than cumulative experiences over time - related to the peak end rule)
- Presence bias (we find it hard to delay gratification - or imagine future pain)

People in sales and service are professional decision-makers. In every conversation, they have to make a string of micro-choices about the content, form and tone of their language, and they have to do it under pressure. Self-enhancement bias might affect their willingness to flex to customers with different preferences. Confirmation bias will affect what they may or may not decide to talk to customers about, based on the assumptions they're making about them. Recency bias could affect what they bring to the very next conversation, based on the last. In other words, cognitive biases can either be their worst enemy - or one of the most effective tools they have to create empathy and influence.

And you don't have to be talking directly to customers for cognitive bias to affect your work. Cognitive bias has a huge impact on leadership too. Self-enhancement bias might affect our willingness to seek feedback and take on new ways of working. Confirmation bias will affect how honestly we engage with the reality of what's happening on the front line and whether our ethos and service principles really are showing up.

Recency bias could lead you to extrapolate an organisation-wide problem (or success) from a single recent experience, or condemn an employee in your head because they just made one mistake.

LEADERSHIP HACKS: COGNITIVE BIAS

i) Declutter decisions
Start becoming aware of how cognitive bias shows up in your leadership. This will help you to think more carefully about the decisions you're making, by clarifying your understanding of what's really going on beneath all the habits in your head. So, whenever you have a decision to make, take the time to take a step back, assimilate all the information before coming to a conclusion, and challenge any biases that may be influencing your thoughts.

ii) Team vision
Are biases clouding the way you lead your people? Look at every member of your team and ask yourself the following questions:

- What do I believe to be true about each person?
- What conclusions have I drawn?
- What assumptions have I made?
- What meaning have I attached to create those assumptions?
- What data did I select to create these assumptions?
- Was I looking at the whole picture or did I miss something?
- Are there any other conclusions or beliefs I could have adopted if I had looked at the bigger picture?

iii) Feedback is a gift
Ask for feedback about biases you may be demonstrating - be open, remain curious and suspend judgement. All feedback is a gift, even when it is poorly wrapped! You may not like it and it may be uncomfortable, but there is value there nonetheless. Regardless of the other person's motivations for giving you feedback, there is always the opportunity to learn something about yourself, and showing that you're accepting feedback as a leader demonstrates the kind of learning mindset you want to see show up in your people (there's more on this to come in Chapter 6).

⚡ CRACK THE CODE: FLEXING

i) Flex at home
Ask your team to start by practising flexing in their personal lives – some of the best insight comes closer to home. Challenge them to discuss these questions in pairs:
- How different are people in your family and friendship groups to you?
- Where are the similarities?
- Can you assign them to a 'preferences profile'?
- What exact ingredients make up the chemistry between you and your partner or best mate?
- When you have arguments, which preferences are clashing?

ii) Customer types
Ask your team to get into the habit of noting down the flex type of each customer who they speak or interact with today. Get together to discuss the results.
- What's the most common type?
- Which do they find most challenging?
- What changes have they had to make to adjust their preferences?
- How difficult did they find it and how did it work?

iii) Flex forecasting
Split the group into their relevant flex types. Tell each group that they are going to prepare and deliver a weather report - but it will be in the style of the flex preference they are least like. They have ten minutes to prepare and then present the forecast to the rest of the group. They should act like that flex preference while planning the weather report as well as presenting it.

Debrief the activity by asking:
- How did it feel to plan the presentation in that style?
- What were your energy levels like?
- What did you learn?

Then ask your team to list all the strengths of the opposite flex type and the ways they can connect with this type of customer more – what would they need to do?

iv) Bias hunting
Ask your team members to partner up and honestly consider what biases they have created about their customers, team members and colleagues. Ask them to discuss: if you imagined that you were meeting those people for the first time, in a neutral setting, how might you treat them differently?

v) Bias in action
There are over 180 cognitive biases, so ask the team to research other biases that could impact how they communicate, make decisions and think about situations. Reflecting on a recent customer conversation, get the team to try to pull apart the biases that may have been at work.
- How many can they name?
- When did they kick in and why?
- What were the facts that seemed to support them at the time?
- Which ones were there from the start?
- What could you have done differently to reduce their power?

Open the discussion back up to the group so you can compare the most common and corrosive biases, and pool solutions.

BEHAVIOUR 4: PAYING IT FORWARD

Watching the Jamaican relay team win 4x100m gold at the 2016 Rio Olympics was a beautiful experience. As Asafa Powell, Yohan Blake, Nickel Ashmeade and of course Usain Bolt flew around the track in a mere 37.27 seconds, it was a vision of immaculate teamwork - hard to see where one runner stopped and another began.

Now imagine if Powell had suddenly flung the baton over his shoulder and sloped off for a coffee break. Or Ashmeade had sprinted in the opposite direction as fast as he could when Blake tried to pass it on.

Or Bolt had denied the very existence of the baton, swapping his signature 'lightning bolt' pose for a 'not-my-responsibility mate' shrug.

That's exactly what happens in customer conversations, hour upon hour. Baton-passing gets turned into buck-passing as people try to shift the responsibility for a customer's problem onto another person or department as soon as they can. I see this happen time and again in three main ways:

- common enemy syndrome
- lack of clarity
- box-ticking.

Common enemy syndrome occurs when someone tries to build rapport with the customer on the basis of blaming someone else in the business. I saw this happen recently in a major national retailer. A customer had ordered some shopping through 'click and collect' then gone to a store to pick it up. The store had no idea where it was, so the customer called the helpline. The call handler's screen said it was definitely there, so he asked the customer how hard the staff at the store had looked, admitting conspiratorially that sometimes they can't be arsed. Of course, he didn't build rapport - he just eroded the customer's trust in the business as a whole.

Lack of clarity happens because someone is trying to avoid accountability. The idea goes that if they give a customer a vague answer rather than a firm promise, then they can't be accused of breaking it. This is happening whenever you hear a conversation saying things like "This might happen - but ring us back if it doesn't", or "Pop back into the store if you get stuck." It's a sure-fire way to make a customer feel confused, disempowered and insecure.

Finally, box-ticking means doing the bare minimum, rather than going the extra mile to make sure any future problems are solved on your watch. Perhaps a team taking a customer's details only needs to get the first line of an address to fill in their form. However, if the delivery team require the postcode for their sat nav system, they're only transferring the effort down the line.

And that's a problem, because our research shows that people hate repeating their stories and having to call back. In a large-scale study for a national supermarket, we found that customers were 3.3 times more likely to score a CSAT 1 (basically, the rock-bottom level of customer satisfaction) on their second contact.

To help your people to pay it forward, you have to engage their imaginations so that they can step into the customer's shoes and predict any problems in advance. You have to motivate them to care about doing a brilliant handover. You have to foster that permission culture that allows them to step out of process and provide an experience tailored to each individual's needs.

But you may also have to take a long hard look at the way your organisation works. These three behaviours - common enemy syndrome, lack of clarity and box-ticking - may be a natural response in a siloed organisation. The team taking the customer's details may not even know that the delivery team needs the postcode. The fault may lie deeper in the structures and processes of the business, and it could be time for some tough truth-telling with your Board.

 ## BRAIN BYTES: THE UNHOLY TRINITY

Yves Morieaux has a problem with modern management techniques. As a senior partner in the Boston Consulting Group and director of the BCG Institute for Organization, he's worked closely inside the world's top businesses. And he claims that what he calls the "holy trinity" of twenty-first century management practice - clarity, measurement and accountability - is eroding our ability to co-operate. "You know, clarity, accountability, measurement were OK when the world was simpler," he declared in a 2015 TED Talk that has been viewed 1.7 million times.[35]

---

35 https://www.ted.com/talks/yves_morieux_how_too_many_rules_at_work_keep_you_from_getting_
things_done/

"But business has become much more complex." Morieaux's teams have measured the evolution of complexity in business and discovered that it is much more difficult today to attract and retain customers and to create value. And so they find that structures, processes and systems multiply.

"You know, this drive for clarity and accountability triggers a counterproductive multiplication of interfaces, middle offices, coordinators that do not only mobilise people and resources, but that also add obstacles," he complains. "And the more complicated the organisation, the more difficult it is to understand what is really happening. So, we need summaries, proxies, reports, key performance indicators, metrics. So people put their energy in what can get measured, at the expense of cooperation. And as performance deteriorates, we add even more structure, process, systems. People spend their time in meetings, writing reports they have to do, undo and redo."

Based on our analysis, teams in these organisations spend between 40 and 80 per cent of their time wasting their time, but working harder and harder, longer and longer, on fewer and fewer value-adding activities. This is what is killing productivity - what makes people suffer at work.

His answer? Strip back process, strip back middle-management, strip back complex systems. In other words, foster a climate where you pay things forward and think about how you can reduce everyone's workload, rather than continually pushing them back and adding to the endless organisational red tape.

⚡ CRACK THE CODE: PAYING IT FORWARD

i) Brilliant batons
Working in small groups, team members identify all the 'baton changes' or shifts in responsibility that they regularly make with other departments, either receiving the baton or passing the baton on. Take each baton change and consider how they would apply each of the following behaviours specifically to it:

- give appropriate acknowledgement
- reassure the customer
- signpost and set up
- own it
- summarise for clarity
- confirm next steps.

Use the concept of the baton by asking each group to pass their views to another group (rotate or swap), who will then represent the views to the wider group.

ii) No wiggle room

The most successful people take time to think about their performance and set themselves stretching goals. But 'big picture goals' are often imprecise, and their ambiguity creates wiggle room for people to rationalise failure. A black and white goal, by contrast, is all-or-nothing. So a precise goal: 'In every customer conversation today I will pay it forward brilliantly' is more powerful than a goal with wiggle room: 'I will improve the way I pay it forward.'

At the end of the working week, ask your team to stop and take a few moments to think about what has gone well and what could have gone better. Now ask them to set 'no wiggle room' goals and the process they will use to achieve this goal. Ask them to 'advertise their change' by sharing this plan with a colleague or line manager. Use the same time next week to ask them to review their plans and see how they did.

iii) Swap shop

Ask your team to record examples of paying it forward well and the impact it had. In your next team meeting, swap stories and share the good stuff. Create a 'bank' of pay it forward statements that the team can draw from in the future.

iv) Social proof

Social proof is a type of conformity. When a person is in a situation where they are unsure of the correct way to behave, they will often look to others for cues concerning the correct behaviour. One way to do this is by looking to people who do things well ('bright spots') and emulating their behaviour. This means that finding the bright spots is a great way to ensure change sticks. So, identify your top performer in terms of paying it forward and ask them to share examples of what they do.

v) Transforming conversations
Run a mini session with your people. Ask them for examples of when common enemy syndrome, lack of clarity and box-ticking may happen and why. Get them to think about the impact this will have on them as a team, the customer and the business as a whole. Establish what you could do as a team right now to ensure you pay it forward brilliantly!

 CRUNCH TIME: TEST YOUR BEHAVIOURS

Run an inspiring, energising meeting with your team to assess your collective progress. First, split them into four groups, then present each team with a customer scenario that reflects conversations that happen frequently.

- Ask each team to think about how they would apply the four behaviours - advocating, using effortless language, flexing, paying it forward - to their scenario.
- Get each team to 'real play' the scenario, with you as a leader playing the customer.
- Tell the other groups that they have an imaginary remote control, which they can use to pause the action. If they see something not quite right, they can pause and coach their peers on what they could do to make the conversation even better.
- Discuss what you discovered in terms of strengths and weaknesses.

Next, set each group the task of focusing on a particular behaviour.

- Ask them to think about the positive impact each behaviour would have on the customer and the business.
- Then ask them to brainstorm ideas for how they could collectively improve their use of that behaviour, and present those ideas back to the group.

How's that behaviours gap looking? Starting to close up? Then it's time to add three more into the mix...

>_ SOURCE CODE: CHAPTER 4

In today's fast-moving digital economy, nice is not enough - customers want an experience that feels human but also easy. The good news is that there are four behaviours that drive a high service experience across all types of business:

1. Advocating: demonstrate that you are on the customer's side by using genuine acknowledgement, accepting accountability and explaining the action you're going to take to solve their issue now.
2. Effortless language: climate is built on conversations, and conversations are built on language. Effortless language conveys positivity, accountability and the feeling of ease.
3. Flexing: we should treat others how they like to be treated, not how we do. Great service people possess the skill of overcoming their cognitive biases and flexing to others, adapting their language in a way that best resonates.
4. Paying it forward: there is nothing more frustrating than being passed from pillar to post around an organisation. Instead you need handovers that feel connected, so that the customer's issue is firmly owned and future issues are headed off.

CHAPTER 5: BLURRED LINES

WHAT'S UP, DOC?

Whenever I have to go and see the doctor, I always experience a bit of anxiety. I'm not necessarily anxious because I'm worried I'm seriously ill. More often than not, I'm nervous because I want to make sure the doctor's going to make the right diagnosis. Because, friendly as my GP is, I never quite trust that he makes the effort to get to the bottom of what's going on.

In my view, there are usually lots of little piece of information that could help Doctor Rao to understand what's happening in the ever-mysterious, vastly complex galaxy known as Sally. Sure, my temperature might not be high right this moment, but it was definitely at fever pitch for a long stretch during the night. Also, weirdly, the same thing happened three nights ago… and on both those days I ate prawns! Ah, but then it also happened two weeks ago, and I hadn't eaten prawns then, so that may or may not be significant. Also, I have this stubborn patch of eczema on my upper arm. And then there's the thing with my toes…

You get the gist. In my mind, my situation is entirely unique. It's wreathed around with dozens of bits of data. I know that some of that data might not be relevant, but if my doctor doesn't know it all - and from experience I know he won't just neglect to ask for it, he'll try to shut me down mid-way through my download - how can I be sure that he hasn't missed the crucial detail that will unlock the truth?

I've already googled my symptoms and found a dozen things it could be scattered across medical forums and blogs and pharmaceutical websites. But now what I need is the human touch: a real person who can synthesise all this information, listen to the tone of my voice, ask questions and finally make the genius diagnostic leap that no bit of technology can.

In short, my five-minute GP appointment is pretty stressful for us both. I'm trying to tell doc everything that's happening in my life, while he's trying to make a reasonable shot at a diagnosis from a couple of factors, prescribe me a cream, then hustle me out of his office before his next needy patient tumbles in.

The last time I sat in his waiting room, making a list of things to mention on my phone, it struck me that many customer conversations play out just like this. A sales or service person talks to customers with similar issues and queries every day, so it's understandable that they might want to cut to the chase and offer the most likely out in the quickest possible time, confident that they know what's going on.

But even if they're right, it's likely that the customer will end up feeling the way I do when I walk out of that surgery: low on confidence, low on trust and low-level anxious. Not exactly a great ending, right?

Which brings us to our next topic: how you're supposed to satisfy your customers when they've already got all the information they could ever want at their fingertips.

FROM PUSH TO PULL

If my twenty-year-old self could jump into the future and watch me swiping and scrolling away on my iPhone, she'd think that my online world was a pretty strange place to hang out. One minute I'm swapping holiday photos with my daughter; the next I'm accepting an invite to a colleague's networking event; the next I'm clicking to buy a 'just in' coat from my favourite brand; then I'm sending a client a link to a video I know they'll love.

Of course, my fortysomething self doesn't see it as strange any more. I just see it as life.

Wherever you look in our digital economy, boundaries are falling over with a silent crash. Working, playing, being creative, shopping, dating, professional networking, spending time with friends: activities that used to belong to specific times and places now happen simultaneously and continuously across a variety of hybrid spaces, on and offline.

And when it comes to how we interact with businesses, the term 'multichannel' doesn't even come close to describing the free-flowing, intuitive, almost subconscious way we research, recommend, complain and buy.

Nowadays, we expect companies to come to us. It's an expectation that's been created over the past couple of decades by a long-tail of lean, digitally-driven startups, where teams sell, serve and market on the same online spaces, each member unquestioningly combining their roles. And, thanks to the power of data-driven algorithms, it feels like these businesses telepathically meet our needs before we even know we have them. When we do reach an actual human, we expect them to replicate the same seamless experience - and add some sort of extra value to reward the fact that we've reached out to a real person instead of a chatbot.

In other words, companies have been forced to sell and serve on the customer's terms. And by 'companies', I mean everyone.

As Dan Pink so brilliantly articulated in his latest book *To Sell Is Human*,[36] a job that was once "a task for slick glad-handers who skate through life on a shoeshine and a smile" has now been outsourced... to everyone. Pink's research reveals that not only are one in nine workers in sales, but we all spend 40 per cent of our work time selling something, whatever our role: "not just objects, but ideas and techniques. We are persuading, negotiating and pitching, like lawyers selling juries on their verdict or public figures selling their personal brand on Twitter."

But as sales becomes more ubiquitous, we've also become more suspicious of people explicitly trying to get us to buy. You only have to open the newspaper in the morning to discover that public trust in institutions and organisations is at an all-time low. From big corporates with dodgy tax practices to politicians with, er, dodgy tax practices, there's a strong sense that the fat cats are out to screw us for all they can get.

36 To Sell Is Human: The Surprising Truth About Moving Others – December 3, 2013 by Daniel H. Pink

For seventeen years, the Edelman Trust Barometer has surveyed tens of thousands of people across dozens of countries about their level of trust in business, media, government and NGOs. This year was the first time the study found a decline in trust across all four of these institutions. In almost two-thirds of the 28 countries they surveyed, the general population did not trust the four institutions to "do what is right", and the average level of trust in all four institutions combined was below 50 per cent[37].

This mistrust extends to sales people. Pink found that 'pushiness' is both the one quality most associated with sales people and the one quality that makes us least likely to buy. This has been compounded by the global recession. Believing that customers buy only on price (and giving in to their own cognitive biases), sales people are becoming increasingly transactional. They focus on money when in fact many of us still enjoy the process of being sold to in a human and personal way.

In the new economy, the lines are truly blurred. Whether you work in a sales, customer service or retail team, customers expect to get some 'value' from the time they invest in every conversation. Sometimes, providing this value might be as simple as offering a bit of useful information. It might involve providing fresh insight into a situation or solving a problem. It often comes from presenting new product possibilities, which can fix a customer's issue or enhance their overall experience.

Top performers in any environment really get this. They provide clarity and make things easy. They are problem finders, as well as problem solvers. They actually develop the customer's thinking - not through objection handling, but by acting as an expert who can offer more than a customer can find by clicking on Guru Google.

Contrast that with the classic 'Sales Through Service' approach, which should really be renamed 'Sales Through Hidden Agenda'. So many people are still trained to play the game of asking all the right questions

37 https://hbr.org/2017/01/survey-peoples-trust-has-declined-in-business-media-government-and ngos

in order to sell the customer a product that most fits their needs - except it just so happens that today that product is the X3000, because they've got shelf-loads that they need to shift. Teams are regularly briefed to manage customer issues in the fastest possible way, in an attempt to reduce the cost to serve - but that defeats the whole idea of service, let alone service that adds real human value.

Best-in-class companies are flipping this approach on its head. They realise that spending the right amount of time on customer conversations, combined with the mindsets and skills discussed in these chapters, will result in value for both the customer and the business. Sure, they know that the fully multi-skilled, flexible frontline person is still a rare creature. But by having and encouraging the right conversations, they'll certainly help develop fewer robots, and more unicorns.

The hard truth at the heart of this issue is very simple. If you are not bringing value to a customer in every sales or service interaction, then quite frankly the customer will not be bringing value to your business. Companies need to start thinking of their 'cost centres' as 'value centres'; value begets value, while cost begets cost.

We've even come up with a name that captures this new approach to sales and service - the Value Experience (VX™). But you don't need a trademark to understand the basic principles and begin to reap the rewards. I guarantee - if you start to talk about value with your colleagues and teams, rather than profit and cost, it will sow the seed of a change in attitude that is long overdue.

Let me share a quick story. I have been a customer of a large telco for years now and have had little need to contact them apart from when I need an upgrade. But then recently I lost, for some unknown reason, all of my photos on my phone. You can imagine my angst. Those precious snaps of Archie's drum solo! Those deeply embarrassing but much-treasured memories of nights out! I called my phone supplier and was met with indifference. The attitude was firmly 'there's nothing we can do'. However, at the end of the call the woman proceeded to tell me about their free, cloud-based back-up service. What the hell? I could have made sure there were copies of all my photos on the cloud? Why on earth had someone not realised that this service would have been valuable to me, and told me about it before it all messed up? If the right questions had been asked in previous calls, someone could have rooted out the information that photos are the most important thing I use my phone for, outside of work. It was a missed opportunity for the telco to build my loyalty to the brand. Instead, I left disappointed and feeling imprisoned in a contract I now wanted to leave.

So, what sort of behaviours can help you win in this new mixed-up sales landscape? How can you provide a seamless personalised purchasing experience, establish trust and still add the sort of human value that a piece of computer code, however smart, can never replicate?

It's time to add three more, sales-oriented behaviours into the mix.

BEHAVIOUR 5: FINDING YOUR KILLER QUESTION

Real curiosity is a rare commodity (more about that in Chapter 6). How often, as a customer, do you feel that someone is asking questions in order to truly root out your unique needs and issues, rather than asking questions so they can fit you into a spreadsheet box?

Anyone who works in sales and service will ask dozens of questions every day. Because of this, most training programmes will offer up multiple question techniques and reams of sample questions to use in their conversations. In our new sales landscape, that isn't enough. Our research shows that questions are not made equal. In fact, the types of questions that have the biggest impact on customer experience differ dramatically from business to business. For example, in our work with a nationwide DIY store, we discovered that one of the key factors that distinguished average sales and service performers from high performers was whether they asked literal questions or vision questions. People who asked customers "What would you like your kitchen to be?"

did okay. But people who asked "What is your dream kitchen?" - specifically using 'visionary' language - got much higher sales.

Let me give you another example. In our work with two broadband providers - same industry, different companies – the killer question that drove the biggest uplift in customer satisfaction was different for each. With one business, it was what we call a 'learning question' ("Tell me what is it that you do for a living?") that really got results. For the other, it was an outcome-oriented question ("What would you really like to happen as a result of our call?") that moved the dial.

Old-school sales training will teach you to use the questioning funnel but, in the new economy, that just isn't specific enough. To find the killer questions above, we had to de-code the conversation for each business by listening to hundreds of interactions from both the highest performers and lowest performers, then establish which questions were linked to the right outcome. This gave us a really clear picture of the best questions to train into each team.

You might well be frothing to interrupt me at this point. Hang on there Sally, isn't there a whole armoury of question types that are helpful in different situations? Yes, of course. There is absolutely a baseline of questioning skill needed here (as there is for anything). Understanding the full range of questions in your armoury is still important. But if you want to be one of the companies delivering outstanding customer experience in our complex world, it's no longer enough.

This behaviour boils down to finding the killer questions that are going to drive the difference for your specific organisation. Honing your questioning 'skills' is old hat. Identifying question types is old hat. You need to get personal and find exactly what questions work best for your customers and your business.

BRAIN BYTES: PROBLEM FINDING

Ten years ago, if you wanted to go on holiday, you would have gone to a travel agent. The agent held all the cards. You would have been forced to trust them, and hope they'd get the best holiday for you. Nowadays, of course, we can just go straight to a comparison site online where we can find the best price, information about the destination, and even search customer reviews.

Think about the last product that you bought that was more significant than a grocery item – maybe an item of clothing, a bit of tech or even a car. Did you go online at some point in the process before you decided to part with your cash? If the answer's yes, you're not alone. A 2014 survey from Pew Research Center found that 89 per cent of people now research online before buying.[38] For service and sales staff, this means that today, the customer is nearly always a step (or three) ahead of you.

So, it's no longer enough for front line staff to see their role as solving problems, because customers can find most solutions on their own. How many times have you "just googled it?" Knowing this, companies might decide to take a purely functional, order-taking approach; but then they run the risk of the customer ending up with the wrong product or the wrong information, or missing out on things that could make a difference to them personally.

So, what do your customers really want from a real live human conversation?

An expert. Someone who can help them think about their problem in fresh and revealing ways, and who can identify problems they didn't know they even had. According to the Edelman Trust Barometer, consumers consistently rate experts as the most trusted spokespeople: more than CEOs or celebrities.[39] There's a scientific reason for this. Neuroscientist Greg Berns found that the decision-making centre of our

38 http://www.pewinternet.org/2014/02/27/about-this-report-4/
39 http://www.edelman.com/trust2017/

brain slows or even shuts down while we are receiving advice from an expert.[40]

If you're not giving them those value-added factors, they may as well shop online.

I am clearly the world's worst nightmare for any sales assistant or customer service advisor. When I go shopping with my daughter, she begs me not to make a scene or complain. I once walked into a large electrical retailer to buy a TV (I know nothing about TVs) and found myself trying to choose between a Panasonic and a Samsung. To my eyes, they appeared to have the same screen size, the same tech specs, the same everything, but one was £50 more expensive than the other. While I was trying to work out what I was supposed to be getting for the extra fifty quid, a spotty 16 year old sauntered over. Knowing this was doomed, but willing to give it a try, I asked him: "So what's the difference?" With heart-sinking inevitability, he got out both of the product tickets and began to stare at them with a frown.

"I'm going to stop you there, mate," I said. "I can read. If all you're going to do is recite the product specification, you need to go and find someone who can actually help." I'm sure you'll have experienced something similar in a British store. It's a recipe for retail rage. All this kid needed to do was ask what was important to me; as it turns out, one of the TVs had a much softer colour while the other had very bright, sharp contrast, so if only he'd been curious about what mattered to me – which was picture quality - he'd at least have known what to go and ask a more knowledgeable colleague.

In an interesting coda to this story, I walked into the same electrical retailer a few years later to buy a laptop for my daughter. All I knew was she needed one for school; I was fairly certain that it didn't need to do a lot, so if I could get one for under £200 - happy days. But there were shelves and shelves of the things, so where to even start? I tried one assistant and it was the same scenario - he starts giving me the product specs without pausing to ask me what I'm actually looking for.

---

40 http://www.ccnl.emory.edu/greg/

Next assistant, the same. I finally happened upon a mobile manufacturer sales guy who happened to be visiting the store - he didn't even work for the retailer and wasn't an expert in laptops, but he'd seen my plight and come over to see if he could help. After asking a couple of questions about what I needed the laptop for, he quickly dismissed one - you can't put Microsoft Office on that and she'll need Word for school - then recommended a basic, inexpensive model as she'd probably need to upgrade in a couple of years anyway.

What is it for? That was my killer question, but it took a hell of a lot of time and effort to find someone who was willing to ask it. The outcome would have been even better if my mobile guy had been an expert - he just about happened to have enough knowledge to cobble together an answer that worked - but expertise wasn't the defining factor for success in this scenario. As so often, that lay with asking the right question.

So, front line staff need to evolve from being problem solvers to being problem finders. They need to be able to suss out hidden problems and provide just the right solutions. It's the old 'unknown unknowns' conundrum; as Steve Jobs summed it up in an interview with Forbes: "A lot of times, people don't know what they want until you show it to them."[41]

How? Look down the road ahead and anticipate future problems the customer might face. Curate information, sorting the wheat from the chaff and making it easy for them to make decisions. Don't assume that they know your organisation's products and services inside out, or that you know everything you need to know about them either.

Try to and identify any knowledge gaps you might have and plug them, by chatting with or observing knowledgeable colleagues. And do some research of your own to increase your expertise.

---

41 https://www.forbes.com/sites/chunkamui/2011/10/17/five-dangerous-lessons-to-learn-from-steve-jobs/#
   58f44ecd3a95

⚡ CRACK THE CODE: FINDING YOUR KILLER QUESTION

i) Spot the difference

Set your team the challenge to uncover the most useful questions for your particular customers in your particular industry right now.

- Talk to your highest performers about the questions they ask customers.
- Ask the same of your lower performers and compare the difference.
- Get everyone to apply the questions that the high performers use and see the difference.

ii) Killer questions

As a leader, you will know what questions work really well with your customers and how to phrase them perfectly. Fine-tune a couple of 'killer questions' that you would like your team to start using (such as the vision question that worked so well for our DIY store).

Write one of these killer questions up on the flipchart and list your team members' names underneath. Set the 'question of the day' challenge, asking them to use this question as much as possible today. Each time they use the question they should come and put a tick by their name. The person with the most ticks by their name at the end of the day wins a prize.

At the end of the day, talk to the team about how asking this question has helped and the impact it had on the customer.

iii) Customer safari

Ask your team to ring three companies whose service you would like to assess - maybe include a competitor.

Their objective is to assess the effectiveness of the questions that are asked. Before they ring, get them to think about what they're expecting to happen, and jot down three words to describe it.

After they have rung, ask them to think about what really happened. Get them to jot down three words that describe it and compare these to the words they wrote before. Use these questions to debrief:

- How effective was the questioning?
- Did they establish what you really needed?
- Did they problem find?

What have they learnt? What could they apply to their own conversations... or avoid?

iii) Learning by teaching
Introduce the concept of problem finding to the team. Explain that they need to be able to suss out a problem that someone doesn't even know they have (yet) and provide a solution(s), and share the science and the concepts you've learnt about the above.

Now look for two volunteers who will design a mini-training session to run in a team meeting. Set them the objective of 'developing the team's problem finding abilities'. After this session, the team can come back to you with examples of how they've helped customers understand problems they didn't even know they had (specific to the particular product). As their leader, make sure you support them through the design process and how they might facilitate the session.

iv) Problem pairs
Ask your team to think about ways they could problem find with customers. Ask each person to commit to one small change that will make a big difference. Get people to pair up with an accountability buddy – who will hold the other person to account for their commitment and discuss with them what difference it is making every few days.

BEHAVIOUR 6: LINKING

Imagine you've just walked into a room of people with a digital TV package to sell. You go up to the first person and ask them what they love to watch on the box.

"Oh, I'm a big sports fan," they say. "Ah!" you reply. "So you love watching sports, what you need is this..." Once you've made the sale, you move on to the next person and ask them what their favourite sort of programme is. "I'm into boxsets," they say. "Political stuff like *House of Cards*." "Ah!" you reply. "So you're into *House of Cards*, what you need is..." Once you've made the sale, you move on to the next person and ask about their televisual poison of choice. "I'm a sucker for soaps," they admit. "Ah!" you reply. "So you're a sucker for soaps, what you need is..."

You get the idea. This is a version of a real exercise we did with one of our clients, a huge multinational digital TV and broadband provider, to help improve the sales rates and satisfaction levels of their customer conversations. The behaviour it demonstrates may seem simple, but it's also incredibly powerful. It's called linking.

Linking statements are a litmus test of relevance. They're the moment when you demonstrate the link from the solution, be it a sales solution or a service solution, back to the customer.

How many times have you heard someone trot out a statement in a service conversation like: "Well, what our service process is..."? The inference beneath the words is: "You can't have what you want", or "Here's what I need to do". Or how about, in a sales conversation, "Let me tell you what it is that we do..." The inference here is: "Here comes the sales pitch you don't really want to listen to!" That's not it. It doesn't feel easy. It doesn't feel effortless. And it isn't really helping the customer.

Linking helps you to turn this 'me, me, me' approach on its head. It allows you to use the information the customer has given you to link to your own solution, by saying things like "So you're looking for..." or "You mentioned earlier that..." When we hear those sort of statements, we have really high trust that the next thing coming out of that person's mouth will be somewhere on the spectrum from good to awesome.

Need some more examples?

Try starting a conversation with "the yellow widget has got the best battery life" and you'll probably send your poor customer to sleep. But start with a linking statement - "So, Mohammad, you said you love to travel, and you said battery life was important to you, so what we've got for you is the yellow widget, because the yellow widget's got the best battery life" - and you've engaged him, shown you're listening, said something true and primed him to expect that the next thing you say will be relevant.

Talking of batteries, as a busy woman who is always running between meetings, I am constantly out of battery. I can't even count the number of times I've had to buy a USB cable in town. It's always the same scenario: I jump out of a taxi, I've got 10 per cent battery life on my phone, I've got a client call in five minutes, I have no idea where to find a plug, and I haven't got a USB cable for my laptop. So, I run into Maplin's, flapping like only I can flap, grab the USB charger, and go up to the till. Except last time, the guy behind the till said: "You look like a lady who runs about town quite a lot." "How can you tell?" I replied. "The blisters? The sweat patches? The bird's nest hair?" "Do you know that we have these little battery packs that are ready charged?" he diplomatically replied. "Shall I stick one of these in your bag?"

It's that easy. Notice what's going on with the customer, ask a question, find a solution, link it back to what the customer has told you... and not just make a sale, but solve a problem they might have been struggling with, undiagnosed, for years.

In a service context, instead of saying "How about Thursday?" you could swap in a linking statement: "So Jane, you're looking for a more convenient delivery time from me today, so I can do Thursday."

Again, you're alerting them to the fact that what you're about to say is important and relevant. You're leading with them, not you. And even if you can't offer them a more convenient delivery time, chances are they'll accept that situation and still be satisfied with the conversation. As I said: simple, but disproportionately powerful.

🧠 BRAIN BYTES: LEADING WITH THE CUSTOMER

Remember that gap we stumbled upon in Chapter 1? The gap between business leaders who want to put the customer first, and their customers, who feel like they're bottom of the pile? Well, leading with the customer is one of the most direct strategies for closing that gap. It's what the 'being customer-centric' service principle looks like in action.

Leading with the customer involves truly listening and being curious about their needs. It's about operating to the customer's agenda, rather than your own - while also balancing the needs of the business around risk, cost and reputation.

In customer conversations, especially when there is a script or a repetitive element involved, it's easy to fall into the trap of operating on autopilot - or 'sleepwalking', as I like to call it. When we sleepwalk, we stop noticing and listening, and often allow the process to take over rather than focusing on what the customer is saying in the moment and trying to 'problem find' what they really need. It happens in those moments when the conversation stops feeling human and when that happens, from the customer's perspective, they may as well be talking to a chatbot.

To lead with the customer, we have to become expert listeners - and listening is one of the hardest skills in the world. Lots of people say they'd like to become a better public speaker, more confident and articulate, but how many times have you heard someone say they want to be a better listener? Not as often, I bet - which is a shame, considering that some neuroscientists suggest that listening releases the same chemicals in your brain as being loved.

There's so much about being human that is associated with being listened to. Empathy, connection, acceptance - most of the really big things we want from life start with listening. So, if you're good at it, you're in a position to fulfil one of our most basic human needs. Listening is a true superpower, all the more so because it is so rare. Refraining from judgement and creating a safe space for sharing is one of the best gifts you can give another person (and it works wonders in your personal life too - believe me!).

From a functional point of view, it also allows you to really assess the needs of the customer and gain all the information you need to diagnose their situation and reach the best outcome.

So how can you demonstrate to the customer that you're leading with them in mind?

Once you've really listened, you'll have a pretty clear picture of their requirements. All you need to do now is find them the solution that best meets their needs and position that in a way that demonstrates this. Let's look at an example.

"Mr Smith, it's really very important to me that I find you a holiday that meets all your needs. So, you mentioned earlier that you've been extremely busy with work this year and the most important thing for you is to relax and to unwind. Well, I've a fantastic holiday for you that will allow you to do just that. It's very quiet, just twenty rooms in total, it has its own private beach and beautiful gardens, and there's a full butler service so you don't even need to lift a finger if you don't want to. You're going to have so much time to relax and read that book you mentioned."

You know that you're leading with the customer if, after each of your interactions, you can answer the following questions with a resounding yes: Has the customer's life improved by the solution I offered? And is the customer in a better place at the end of our conversation than they were before it even began?

We want the customer to leave the conversation feeling loyal to our brand. We want them to feel satisfied, having truly experienced a human conversation - something they just can't get from a quick google online.

⚡ CRACK THE CODE: LINKING

i) Linking buddy

This is a great opportunity to encourage your team to use the 'advertise the change, assess the impact' strategy I introduced in Chapter 4. Ask them to:

- Tell a colleague that they're going to make a change to their conversation, using linking statements
- Choose their favourite style of linking statement
- Use the statement in the next five interactions
- Notice the difference it makes
- Report what they discovered back to the same colleague.

ii) The big debate

Split your team into two groups and hold a parliamentary style debate. Have one group debate for the statement below and one group against: 'Linking makes a difference to customer conversations.'

Give each group two minutes to present their argument. Once they have presented, the debate can begin. It will need facilitating, but the group will generally come to a quick realisation that this is a critical behaviour for all sorts of reasons.

You can repeat this debate format, but using other revealing statements and behaviours to provoke discussion. One of my favourites is: 'Focusing on the conversation first, then the process, gets the best result.'

iii) Leading questions

Encourage your people to do these things:

- Listen to or reflect on five conversations, answering the questions Did the solution I offered really match the customer's need? Has the customer's life improved as a result of the solution I offered? Is the customer in a better place after our interaction than they were before it began?

- Use curious questions to uncover what the customer's real needs are; build up a questioning bank and use them in each conversation.
- Look for opportunities to use the information provided to link what the customer is looking for to the solution they have provided.

iv) Product puking
Set up a discussion called 'product puking' - this happens when sales and service people list loads of product or service features to customers that have no relevance to their need. Ask the team to think about the impact of 'product puking' on the customer and what strategies they could use to avoid this happening.

Introduce the concept of linking to the team, using some examples of what customers say in a conversation and how they can link to this information using linking statements like "Which means that...which gives you...you said X was important to you". It would be helpful to use a recorded call or a mystery shop to really bring this to life.

In pairs, ask your team discuss how they could now use what they have learnt about linking to make customer conversations even stronger. Share all ideas, and encourage people to use their imagination.

v) Real play
'Real-play' a customer conversation as a team, stopping and rewinding to reword until, together, you have come up with the perfect way to link what the customer said to what the service person has said.

Gain commitment from all team members to use linking in future. Focus on this in uncoaching conversations and look out for people doing it well, sharing stories of success.

vi) Have you got linking talent!
To prepare for this activity, buy a couple of buzzers - they're really cheap

online. Prior to this session, create a number of customer scenarios that will provide an opportunity for team members to demonstrate the behaviour of 'linking'.

Explain to your team that they will be put on the spot and asked to come up with linking statements based on what you tell them. Get each person to line up and start reading scenarios out one by one. If they stumble, pause or don't use a linking phrase, buzz them and they are out. Keep going until you have a clear winner - and have fun!

BEHAVIOUR 7: ONE MORE THING

We all like happy endings. One more thing combines problem finding and the peak end rule to help you deliver the most effective ending possible to a customer conversation.

Our role model here is Columbo (or maybe Jimmy McNulty, if you want to bring it more up to date). The skill here is, once you've asked all your questions, to make a point of ensuring that you've discovered every last detail by asking - yes, you guessed it - one more thing.

You see, the downside about being a human, instead of a robot, is that we can't be at the top of our game all the time. Three pm on Wednesday means nothing to an algorithm, but that post-lunch hump-day slump can have a big impact on the human mind. But although we can't always be at our best, we can use the same behaviours every time.

That's important because our Blue Sky research shows that the highest performers in sales and service are those who follow the same process every time. It's like a safety net - the behaviours will deliver the right customer experience even if the person behind them isn't feeling 100 per cent. If you think you've come to the end of your question-asking part of the conversation, but you make a point of double-checking by asking one more thing, that means you know you've got all the information you need to present the right solution, whatever the customer scenario happens to be.

One more thing works in many different environments, and a really great example that works for all of them goes like this: "Mary, is there anything else that's really important to you that you think I should know about?" One more thing. That's it.

BRAIN BYTES: THE PEAK END RULE

Science has helped us understand the importance of the first magic minute of a conversation, we've asked our killer questions, found the problem, linked to customer needs and hopefully presented a solution that the customer loves. But now is not the time to take our foot off the gas; we need to understand how to leave that conversation 'on a high.'

Our brains are full of illusions, errors of judgement that interfere with what we consider to be rational thoughts. One of the masters at exposing these errors is the Nobel-Prize winning psychologist Daniel Kahneman (him again), and one of his most famous discoveries is the peak end rule. The peak end rule stipulates that people judge an experience largely based on how they felt at its peak (i.e. its most intense point) and at its end, rather than based on the total sum or average of every moment of the experience.

This idea was first introduced in a groundbreaking 1993 study titled 'When More Pain Is Preferred to Less: Adding a Better End'[42] by Kahneman and his co-researchers. The first trial saw participants submerge one of their hands in 14°C water for sixty seconds. The second trial saw participants submerge the other hand in 14°C water for sixty seconds, but then keep their hand submerged for an extra thirty seconds, while the temperature was raised to 15°C. The participants were then offered the option of which trial to repeat, and they were more willing to repeat the second trial, even though it meant spending more time exposed to uncomfortable temperatures. Kahneman et al. concluded that "subjects chose the long trial simply because they liked the memory of it better than the alternative (or disliked it less)".

---

42 https://www.jstor.org/stable/40062570

In a 2010 TED Talk, Kahneman used a vivid story to illustrate how the peak end rule works. "[A man told me] he'd been listening to a symphony and it was absolutely glorious music and at the very end of the recording, there was a dreadful screeching sound," Kahneman explained. "And then he added, really quite emotionally, it ruined the whole experience. But it hadn't. What it had ruined were the memories of the experience. He had had the experience. He had had twenty minutes of glorious music. They counted for nothing because he was left with a memory; the memory was ruined, and the memory was all that he had gotten to keep."

So what does this mean for sales and service? It means that how we finish a conversation is extremely important. Even more so when we learn that these peak end memories get stored in our brain at a subconscious level, where they will eventually direct our buying decisions and our attitude towards a company.

Need another example? Imagine that you've gone to see an action movie. The film has amazing special effects but the ending is a bit limp. You probably wouldn't exhort your friends to go and see it, right? Well, relate that to the customer experiences you are creating. You may have given a strong welcome, asked great questions and offered helpful solutions but, unless you pay attention to how you close the conversation, much of your good work will go to waste.

Or think about IKEA. What person in their right mind would return to IKEA after their first trip? You have to trudge around a huge store at a snail's pace, weaving between confused people pushing wonky trolleys loaded with stuff they probably don't even want. You have to search the shelves for ages to find a deconstructed coffee table bearing the name of a Nordic death-metal band. You have to queue for even longer at the checkout and load every last Nnoffkrullen teaspoon onto the conveyer belt yourself. So why on earth do you keep going back? (and you do - IKEA has an incredible loyalty record).

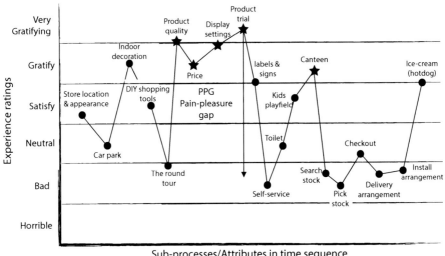

The peaks. IKEA is a genius at creating positive peaks throughout a mostly rubbish experience, from that amazing little ten-foot-square kitchen-lounge display, to the beds your kids bounced on in their dirty wellies, to the tiny free pencils, to the fact that THAT SOFA ONLY COSTS £59.99!!! Or at least that's what the peaks in this graph would represent if they were tracking my average visit. And, of course, there's the end. IKEA has absolutely nailed the end of the peak end rule via the medium of cheap and dirty hot dogs and ice cream. There's probably only one thing powerful enough to obliterate the memory of IKEA's checkout hell, and that's sitting in the playground outside with 30p-worth of sugar and chemicals dribbling down your chin. If Daniel Kahneman made interiors stores…

Peak endings don't have to be dramatic. They can be achieved using really small finishing touches that make people smile, and they work in any environment. Having trained 9000 engineers sent out to work in customers' homes, we discovered as part of our conversation analytics that the top performers displayed one modest but consistent behaviour: they wiped down the bathroom when they left the house. Thanks to this insight, there are now many more bathrooms around the country that get the lemon fresh treatment when an engineer visits - and many more happy customers as a result.

And yet the single most used phrase at the end of a service experience is "Is there anything else I can help you with?" That's not it! That is not a peak. You're going to have to try harder if you want to match that 30p ice cream. I have been a customer of First Direct for twenty years and at the end of every service interaction, the First Direct employee would always refer back to some nugget of personal information I'd let slip. If I'd said that I was driving home, they'd finish with "I hope you get home safely". They were always on the lookout for little conversational gifts that they could use to create a memorable ending. And it worked.

 ## LEADERSHIP HACKS: ONE MORE THING

Try asking 'one more thing' at the end of every meeting to make it a part of your climate. Use the same language every time - "and now I'm going to yup, you got it, ask one more thing: is there anything else that's important to you that you think I should know about?" This doesn't just help build the habit. It demonstrates that the seven skills we've explored throughout the past couple of chapters can help improve engagement in every area of the business, not just in customer conversations. And it's a lovely example of a VDA: those small but powerful actions leaders take to model the behaviour they want to see business-wide.

 ## CRACK THE CODE: ONE MORE THING

i) One more reminder
Help your team to find a way to remember to pause, reflect and ask one more thing before they finish a conversation or move onto a new issue. From 'one more thing' cookies to 'one more thing' wristbands, think of some creative, fun ways to embed the ritual in their minds.

ii) Peak irritation
Over the next few days, always add this statement to the end of a conversation with a team member: 'Anything else I can help you with?' (sound a bit disconnected as you say it, rush it with a bored tone). Ensure you do this to at least 75 per cent of the team before running this session.

Then, in your daily team meeting ask: has anyone noticed anything strange about the way I am ending conversations with you? What have you noticed? How did it make you feel? Did you believe I was genuinely enquiring or saying it for the sake of it? What did my tone imply? Then ask them: how do you end conversations with customers? How do you find out if they want to ask you anything else? What impact do you think this has on them?

Explain the concept of 'one more thing' and remind them of 'problem finding' and finding out everything the customer needs up front, which removes the need to ask 'anything else I can help you with?' at the end.

Gain everyone's commitment to stop ending conversations in a disconnected way and to genuinely ensure they have understood the customer's full enquiry up front. As a leader, listen out for people doing this well when coaching this week. Share and celebrate stories of success.

iii) Peak Pictionary
Explain the peak end rule to your team. Working in pairs, ask your team members to reflect on what the peak end rule means in terms of customer conversations. Peak endings should:
- Summarise the next steps and actions.
- Refer to something personal that was given freely by the customer in the conversation
- Bring a little personality to the ending/do something surprising.
- Demonstrate the value that has been added.
- Involve the team member sounding 'happy to have helped'.
- Deliver a peak end whether the outcome is a yes or no to any additional products or services that have been introduced.
- Head future issues off that mean the customer has to contact again.

Now split the team into three groups. Give each group flipchart paper and pens. They have ten minutes to come up with the best suggestions for peak endings to their conversations. They are not allowed to write any words; they can only draw pictures to represent their peak end.

After ten minutes each group should reveal their pictures and explain their peak ends. Award a prize for the best one. Each person should now commit to delivering a new peak end on their next shift and report back.

iv) Peak practice

Ask your people to listen to, or reflect on, their past five customer conversations, through the lens of how strong the ending was. Did it make the conversation feel connected and memorable? Ask them to share their strongest peak ending with the team.

Then, in the next five conversations, get them to ask for feedback from the customer at the end of the conversation: "What could I have done to make this even easier for you today…?" Ask them to share their findings with the team.

CONCLUSION: FINDING YOUR X FACTOR

I'd like to finish this chapter with a story from a national supermarket we worked with, which highlights one final, important lesson about customer experience behaviours.

A customer at one of this supermarket's stores was charged 6p too much for two croissants, several times in a row. He complained to the customer service manager that it kept happening and he needed to sort it out as he didn't have the time to queue up again with his receipt every time. The manager went straight to a solution and gave the customer 'double the difference' for 12p and sent him £2 gift card in the post.

Sounds good, right? Except the customer wasn't pleased at all. He was in fact incredibly frustrated and scored their conversation a CSAT 1. Why? Because the manager had failed to identify the customer's real objective. He didn't want 12p; he didn't even want £2; he wanted the root issue to be addressed so it didn't happen again.

The lesson here is that, although the seven behaviours you've learnt in the past couple of chapters will help make any organisation more customer-focused and more successful at delivering a brilliant customer experience, every business is different. The only way to discover what the specific differentiators of high performance are for your business is to do your research.

Different skills drive higher NPS outcomes in different businesses. For our supermarket manager above, understanding the true objectives of a customer was the behaviour that would have transformed a CSAT 1 into a CSAT 5. For a big telco client of ours that often deals with small businesses, we found the greatest challenge was peeling back all the layers of issues surrounding the initial 'problem', so asking one more thing made the difference between a successful experience and a string of call-backs. And for a national water company, we discovered that their complicated multiple-touchpoint customer experience made paying it forward an absolute priority.

So, it's important to gather data on your own customer conversations and drill down into exactly what's going wrong - and right. If you don't, you might end up sending out an awful lot of gift cards, when you should simply have fixed the code on the till for croissants.

⏱ CRUNCH TIME: TEST YOUR BEHAVIOURS (AGAIN)

Yes! It's time to take another inspiring, energising meeting with your team to assess your collective progress. First, decide to use one of your products or services that you would like to sell more of as a case study.

- Ask everyone to spend 15 minutes creating for themselves the character of a really specific customer who is significantly different from themselves, working out their age, likes, dislikes, context and behaviours (flex types can help here).
- Then ask one third of the room to take on the role of their customer, while one third has to try selling them your chosen product or service, and the other third observes.
- Encourage them to move onto their next customer, speed-dating style, as soon as they have tried or failed to make their sale.

- Swap roles three times so that everyone gets to play customer, employee and observer.
- Return to the whole group to discuss how the behaviours helped, and how the individual nature of different customers changed the way they were used.

Second, create peer-to-peer coaching buddies in your team. Successful people look for feedback and support, so ask your team members to find a coaching buddy from amongst their colleagues. They don't need to be in the same team. Get them to agree how often they will meet and how the relationship will work. Then share with them some things they and their coaching buddy can do:

- Discuss their strengths and development areas. Share ideas on how to work on development areas.
- Share plans for the following week or month.
- Listen in to each other's customer conversations and give feedback.
- Role-play potentially difficult or challenging conversations that need to be had.
- Advertise their changes to each other.

Congratulations! You've set your tone, primed your climate and armed your team with a set of up-to-the-minute behaviours for outstanding sales and service. But there's something else you need to ensure that all this great new work doesn't fade and falter over the months.

Yes, you need transformation glue. Otherwise known as mindsets...

>_ SOURCE CODE: CHAPTER 5

The lines between sales and service have become blurred. Customers expect employees to bring more value than they can get clicking on Google or surfing Amazon.

There are three behaviours that a computer can never replicate. These build trust, make the experience feel personal and help customers unearth problems they never thought they had:

1. Asking the right questions: real curiosity is a rare commodity, and a vital part of the conversation code. But not all questions are equal. Your top performers use killer questions to drive results, and it is these - not old-fashioned training techniques – you need to focus on.
2. Linking: linking statements are a litmus test of relevance. They demonstrate that your people are truly leading with the customer by listening to what is important to the customer and then tailoring the solution accordingly - not listing products or specs.
3. One more thing: this simple yet powerful safety net ensures that you have the right information to present the right solution - and leave the customer with a peak ending.

CHAPTER 6: THE BIG MIND RESET

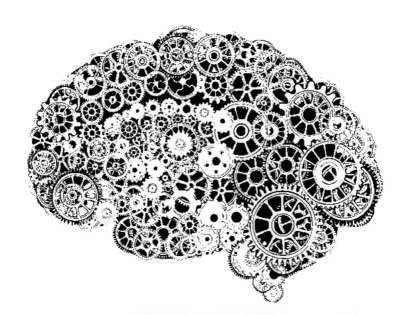

FAIL BETTER

In 1978, a team of American psychologists led by a woman called Carol Dweck offered a group of four-year-olds a choice.[43] The children could either redo a simple jigsaw puzzle they'd been given or have a go at a more difficult one.

Some of the kids opted to stick with the easy puzzle they'd already solved, eager to reinforce their existing ability. Having told the researchers that clever kids don't make mistakes, they wanted to avoid the risk that they might fail. Others, however, seemed bewildered by the question. Why would anyone want to repeat the same jigsaw? The whole point of a puzzle was to make you smarter, wasn't it? Duh. They rolled up their tiny sleeves and got stuck in.

This seminal study marked the early days of a now-flourishing discipline: the science of mindsets. The first group of kids exhibited a 'fixed mindset': a belief that intelligence is a finite resource, which led them to anxiously cling onto what they already had. The second, however, demonstrated a 'growth mindset': a belief that intelligence is built by being challenged, and that the definition of success lies in stretching yourself.

Having a growth mindset has been proved to be a crucial discriminating factor between people who become true experts and those who stay on a plateau. In other words, it distinguished the winners from the losers (although they probably didn't tell the four-year-olds that).

We all like to think we're growth mindset kind of people. But when we really look hard at how we've dealt with the past few challenges in our life, it can be pretty startling to realise how often we cling to, well, to the mindset of a risk-averse four-year-old.

---

43 http://www.unco.edu/cebs/psychology/kevinpugh/motivation_project/resources/dweck_leggett88.pdf

SAND, NOT ROCK

By now we've covered an awful lot of science, seven crucial behaviours, and a whole range of ideas for how to set the tone and build a climate where customer experience can thrive. But without the right mindsets, your whole beautiful transformation project will soon begin to slide.

Your CEO announces an exciting new leadership development programme. Sales and service training is rolled out. There are lots of inspiring workshops and presentations, a sense of excitement, some great early wins, some powerful Symbolic Actions. There's a buzz about the place. You're already planning what you're going to wear to the award ceremony. Then, day by day, week by week, old habits creep back in, energy dissipates and 'business as usual' reasserts itself. That humble but scalding hot little cocktail number (or tux) goes back in the wardrobe. We've all seen it happen; most of us have been right in the depressing thick of it.

So why is it so hard to make the sort of changes I am proposing here stick?

Because a business, unlike computers and algorithms and lovely books with neat numbered lists like this, is essentially chaotic. In the terms of the famous Biblical parable: it's the house built on sand, not rock. Consumers are always changing; technology is always changing; the demands of the market are always changing. This sort of uncertainty makes us feel unsafe, leading us to cling to what we already know and entrench ourselves into a fixed mindset.

Tough talk about 'manning up', 'being resilient' and 'disrupting ourselves' - and this is talk most of us have also heard before, many times - only makes us shut down further. When we hear that, we strap on more mental and emotional armour to protect ourselves from the onslaught, and become ever more scared and stiff. Instead, we need to find ways to damp down our flight-or-fight hormones and stay accountable, curious, agile, present and use our imagination. And to do that, we must learn how to harness the power of mindsets.

MINDSET 1: ACCOUNTABILITY

If I were to tell you that there is a way of thinking that shows up time and time again in the highest performing teams... if I were to tell you that this mindset underpins our ability to be the best that we can be, however we define that for ourselves, in any given situation... I'm guessing that you might quite like to know what it is, right?

But first, a story.

I think I have always been the sort of person who believes that you can achieve anything you want to achieve, if you just put your mind to it. For example, I discovered nightclubs and boys at around the same time as I started 'studying' for my A levels. Not a good combination, as you can imagine; the few lessons I did attend were spent with a Sony Walkman cassette player plugged into one ear. But then, about three weeks before my exams, I thought more about Fresher's Week and student parties, and suddenly decided that I might quite like to get a place at university after all. So, with the mindset that you can achieve anything if you just put your mind to it firmly installed, I set about learning two years' worth of curriculum in three weeks. Much to my parents' surprise and my teachers' indignation, I actually got the grades that I needed to get to university and off I skipped to Fresher's Week and freedom with a smile on my face.

This idea - that mindset has a massive impact on performance - came into sharp focus again a few years later when I was working with quite a large team of sales people. Now, this team had a quite unique task, selling high value products inside customers' homes; a pretty unusual job in a world of online shopping and automated checkouts. There were 500 people in the team, and their leader wanted to drive up their sales performance. Obviously.

However, this team had what we call a very wide performance distribution. At one end of the spectrum, there was a fairly small percentage of really low performers. In the middle, there were an abundance of average performers. But at the other extreme, there was a tiny handful of high performers: six outliers outshining the rest of the group. Understandably, this sales leader wanted to know why. What did these six performers have that everybody else didn't? Was it some unique sales capability that they'd developed over time? Or were they just blessed with that 'gift of the gab' that only certain sales people have?

We set about trying to find out what that X factor was. We took those six high performers and we put them through simulations, interviewed them, assessed every aspect of their performance. And what we found was fascinating. These outliers didn't have much in common at all. They were all bringing an incredibly different and unique way of selling into customers' homes. The only thing that they did have in common was their mindset.

Accountability Ladder
Where do you stand?

Make it happen

Find a solution

Take responsibility

Acknowledge reality

Accountable Behaviours
Things happen because of you

Waiting & hoping

Victim Behaviours
Things happen to you

Blaming others

Making excuses

Wallowing in limiting beliefs

Now, while their peers and colleagues were all operating down at the bottom of this ladder, wallowing in limiting beliefs ("Ah, this job's too hard, I can't do it!") or making excuses ("It's much easier to sell to the Welsh than it is to the Scots" - that's a verbatim quote), or blaming others ("I'd be amazing if my manager was better") or waiting and hoping for the magic wand of success to tap them on the head in the middle of the night... the six high performers were actively operating above the dotted line. They were taking responsibility for their performance and taking action off their own bat, every single day, to improve.

One of them told me that after every single appointment he would drive his car around the corner, sit in there and go through every element of the conversation that he'd just had, working out what had gone well and what had gone badly, and making a change in the moment to his approach so the very next conversation would be different. Another confessed that he was worried about his technical knowledge, so, in the absence of any good training materials, he used to go online in his own time, download technical product specifications and learn them overnight. A third explained that whenever he got a 'rubbish appointment' - the team's name for certain customers that it was really hard to sell to - he would use it as an opportunity to practise a new way of selling that might work. And although most regular team members didn't even bother showing up to those rubbish appointments, he was managing to convert 1 in 10.

In every team, in every business, there are people who think at the bottom of the ladder and people who think up above the dotted line. You don't have to be a genius consultant to work out who your high performers are going to be - just put them in a room, listen to the way they talk to each other, and you'll hear the mindsets shine out without even looking at an Excel spreadsheet.

Now, I could be accused of grossly over-simplifying the link between mindset, behaviour and performance in our neat little ladder. And you might be right. There are swathes of research and evidence out there that make the link between mindset and performance in all sorts of complex and fascinating ways, from the nature/nurture argument right the way through to cognitive behavioural therapy. But although that's all good and true and right, when you've got five minutes to persuade somebody, in the moment, to think differently - to see a different way, to take a different action - this cheeky little ladder works better than anything else I've tried.

It's also incredibly sticky. By that I mean that once you share the accountability ladder with others, it really does spread. I was working with some managers up in Rotherham when one of them came to me after a session and cried: "I love this Sally! I love this ladder! Its brilliant! When I get my team in a meeting and we're all sat around and we're getting a little bit negative, a little bit cynical and struggling to come up with answers, I just get the ladder out and point at it and everybody changes direction in the room." Nature/nurture that.

The ladder seemingly has the power to blast through hierarchy, too. I was once walking through an office when I spotted a PA sitting behind a glass window. A bloke who looked a lot more senior than her walked into the room and started gesticulating, obviously having a rant. The PA just looked at him and pointed at the poster of the ladder behind her head. The guy stopped and stared... then off he walked. In that moment, someone very junior could hold someone very senior to account, without a single word being said.

This little ladder is also incredibly memorable. I was on the phone to somebody the other day who I didn't think that I knew, but he started the conversation by saying, "Actually Sally, we've met before. I was at an event that you were running, where you shared something about mindset. You're the Ladder Lady!" Twenty-five years of performance improvement condensed into two words: Ladder Lady. Brilliant!

And, of course, the accountability ladder doesn't just work for business. I would hazard a guess that everyone who reads this book has got something that they would like to change, something that they would like to be different in their life. Maybe you'd like to get fit or improve a relationship, take on a new challenge or pursue a new dream - but I bet you have something. And I don't believe for a minute that you set out to fail. None of us likes to believe that we're someone who lives 'at the bottom' (of the ladder). But I do think that we have a habit of getting a little bit stuck. From time to time, we will all operate on the bottom rung. I'm sure you can think of a mood hoover in your life - someone who loves to wallow in self-pity, blame everybody else for whatever's going wrong and drag you down too. But every one of us is a mood hoover, sometimes.

The point is, while we're on the bottom rung of that ladder, nothing changes. We don't set out to pursue new challenges while we're telling ourselves "I could never do that". We don't set ourselves new goals while we're telling ourselves "I haven't got the time". We don't make new relationships while we're telling ourselves "It's everybody else's fault". And we definitely don't try to build a new world while we're telling ourselves "It's someone else's problem".

Each and every single one of us needs to make a choice to move above the line if we actually want to make a change. And I believe these eight simple rungs allow us to do that - to represent our way of thinking in a clear graphical form, and to allow us to start to make decisions about the kinds of choices and changes that we want to make.

Once you have got used to thinking in terms of the ladder, it infects everything. Admittedly, it can be a little bit irritating for those around you, but a bit of irritation is a small price to pay for taking responsibility for your life. It takes a lot of guts to be able to look at yourself in the mirror every morning and say: "Everything that happens to me today is all my fault." Wait, what? Yes, okay, there are lots of things that happen to us that are outside of our control. But if you can remain accountable, even in the face of adversity, it will only ever have an incredibly positive effect on your work and your life.

A few years ago I worked with a woman who had been living with cancer for many years. During the time that I worked with her, she learned that the cancer had become terminal, and what she said to me will always stay in my mind. Even in the face of this terrible news, she said that she had come to realise that even though she couldn't control the outcome of her illness, she could certainly control the person that she wanted to be in the meantime. She could certainly control the legacy that she wanted to leave, during the time that she was alive.

Thanks to that woman, I believe that we all have the ability to operate at the bottom or to operate up the top - with no exceptions at all. I believe we can all make a choice to achieve whatever we want to achieve and to be whoever we want to be - whether you define that as passing A levels, changing career, achieving success at work or building relationships. I believe that we truly can get to wherever we want to be, but it all starts with one little question: Where am I on the ladder right now?

LEADERSHIP HACKS: ACCOUNTABILITY

i) Inbox introspection
Print off the last ten emails you sent in your work or home life (or both). As you read through them, reflect on where you were on the accountability ladder with each one. What impact might your actions have had? If you are below the line, consider what you could do to raise accountability.

ii) Change it up
Think about a change you're trying to make in your life right now. Where are you on the ladder, and how could you move yourself up just one or two rungs to start to take some action?

iii) Ladder on your shoulder
In every conversation you have, whether it's with your family, colleagues, team members or customers, just imagine that accountability ladder hovering above you the whole time. Keep asking yourself: where am I on the ladder?

iv) Oh happy day

Recently there was a challenge doing the rounds on Facebook, and it's very simple: stop complaining for a day. For a whole twenty-four hours consciously stop yourself from moaning or complaining about all that stuff that irritates you about life: the milk being off; your phone charge running low; the person eating noisily on the train; the colleague who annoys you; the government and so on. It's not as easy as it sounds but, if you can master this, you're on your way to living above the line.

v) Blame game

Spend a day being on the lookout for moments of blame. This may be blaming yourself or another and see if you can recognise how it was a moment of expelling pain, discomfort or some negative energy. How does it make you feel after? Was it relieving? Does more negative energy creep in?

Then spot it in others - spend the next day noticing when other people use blame. Do you notice some pain or discomfort that preceded their moment of blaming? See the freedom unfold - see what happens as you start to get curious about the experience of blame.

vi) You get the team you deserve

Our teams are a reflection of our leadership. If they are not performing as a team, you need to look at what you need to do more or less of as a leader. Are you waiting for things to happen or blaming others for underperformance? Consider what you yourself could do right now to improve your team's performance.

⚡ CRACK THE CODE: ACCOUNTABILITY

i) Team accountability

Introduce the accountability ladder model to the team. Ask them these questions: when have you been accountable or unaccountable at work? When have you experienced these behaviours and how did they affect the outcome?

In pairs, ask the group to think of an issue or challenge they are currently dealing with. Ask them these questions: what is your current stance? How accountable are you being? What do you want to achieve? Ask them to look at the accountability ladder and practise making distinctions between why they would choose one level over another. What do they need to do differently to move up the ladder?

Next, ask them to consider a customer interaction that was slightly heated, where the customer was frustrated. Ask them these questions: how accountable were you? Were you blaming or making excuses? On reflection, what could you have done differently to have been more accountable?

Ask your team to notice the language they are using in a situation. Their language can indicate where they are on the ladder. Then, ask them to make a choice - to stay where they are, or to make a change to move up a few rungs.

ii) Facetime
Print out the accountability ladder poster size, including all rungs with labels, with the heading; 'How accountable are you?'

Cut out a headshot photo of each member of the team and blu-tack them at the side. When team members ask you questions about potential issues and solutions during coaching, use this poster as a tool, move their photo onto different rungs. Ask questions such as:

- What rung would you be on if that is your full solution?
- Where does that sit on the accountability ladder?
- If you were going to find a full solution and make it happen what would that look like? What would you need to do?
- What will happen if you just wait and hope?

When you overhear accountable behaviour, move the photo of the team member concerned onto the ladder, putting them on the right rung such as 'Acknowledge reality', and give them a thumbs up. If appropriate, you can also move photos to 'Blaming others' or 'Making excuses' when you hear people doing these things. This should be kept fun and light hearted, though. This is a visual tool to get people to become aware about the conversation choices they are making and the things they habitually say and do.

MINDSET 2: CURIOSITY

"I have no special talents; I am only passionately curious." So said Albert Einstein, a man who most of us think of having talents way out of our league. But Einstein didn't believe that his genius lay in his knowledge of physics. He knew it resided in his mindset: the mindset of an explorer, who was committed to delving into every dark corner he came across.

Sales and service people are explorers too: explorers of people. But you often see that curiosity is missing in conversations with customers. Whether you're in a call centre, working in the field or in a retail store, you rarely see enough exploring, either of the customer's needs or of their problem, particularly at the start of a conversation. Teaching front line staff to ask more and better questions certainly can help, as our three behaviours in Chapter 5 demonstrated.

But that's not enough.

We've found that we're actually lacking a mindset of curiosity in life in general. The first place we see this showing up is in our habit of 'passing the information ball'. All too often in conversations involving a group of people, whether that's new mums talking about babies or colleagues talking about a work problem, you'll see them passing information around the group, like they're tossing the 'information ball' from one person to the other but never exploring it in greater detail.

For example, imagine you're having dinner with a group of friends, talking about holidays. One mate says "Oh, I went to Greece last year." Instead of asking "How was it?" or "Where did you go?" her neighbour chips in "I've been there as well!" Then the next friend goes on to describe a great Greek restaurant she's recently discovered, and so on.

That's fine, and we can happily sit there doing this for hours, but we're basically just using each other's comments as a hook to hang our own thoughts on: passing the information ball.

The second way in which we see this showing up - and this is perhaps a little more detrimental - is in our tendency to make assumptions. This happens when people pass us information, but we forget to explore the meaning or intent behind their words. We make assumptions about what's been said and attach our own meaning to it, and then make a judgement about what that person intended.

You see this a lot in relationships at home. If my partner says to me "Are you going to be late again tonight?" I might hear it, then instantly attach meaning to it like 'Oh, he must be annoyed with me for being late for the past four days' - but without exploring it, how do I know? Actually, if I explore it and ask questions about it, what I might find out is that's not what he intended at all. Maybe - gasp - he was trying to be supportive (this little exchange may have played out more than once recently). So, without curiosity, we're constantly attaching meaning and making assumptions, and not accurately interpreting what's being said to us by other people.

Moreover, in a customer service or sales context, it can feel very anti-intuitive to dig deeper into people's needs or look harder for more problems. Our instinct tells us to quickly identify the most glaring issue or the most relevant product, get it sorted for them and move on. After all, don't we both want to get this over as quickly as possible?

But that does not feel great for the customer and a lack of curiosity can lead to all sorts of missed opportunities and lingering problems that will simply get 'paid forward' to some unfortunate colleague. Instead it pays to think like Einstein. Yes, a curiosity mindset works as well for customer experience as it does for theoretical physics, and it can also do wonders for your friendships - not to mention all those little grumpy "are you going to be late again?" miscommunications that crop up in life.

LEADERSHIP HACKS: CURIOSITY

i) Three more questions
Pick a conversation today and force yourself to ask three more questions than you normally would. So, if you bump into someone making coffee in the staff kitchen, don't settle for a "How are you?" / "I'm fine" duet. Go further. "You know, I've never asked where you live. Do you have a long commute?" and "Did you grow up around there then?" You won't just make a better connection in that conversation; you'll learn things that allow you to better relate to that person in future, perhaps even kick off a deeper long-term relationship.

ii) Curiosity Tuesdays
Pick a topic every Tuesday - say, what makes a good leader, or the history of your business's founder - and make it your mission to find out more about it.

iii) Start curious
With every conversation you have for the next week, try to start every response with a question. It'll unlock the information-passing cycle and you'll be surprised by what a difference it makes to the quality of the exchange.

⚡ CRACK THE CODE: CURIOSITY

i) How curious are you?
Gather your team and get them to complete this self-assessment, rating the following statements using a score from 1 to 5, where 1 is 'not like you at all' and 5 is 'very like you'.

1. I can learn almost anything if I set my mind to it.
2. I find it fascinating to learn new information.
3. When I learn something new I would like to find out more about it.
4. I feel frustrated if I can't figure out the solution to a problem so I work even harder to solve it.
5. I enjoy discussing abstract concepts.

6. I work like a fiend at problems that I feel must be solved.
7. Difficult conceptual problems can keep me awake all night thinking about solutions.
8. I brood for a long time in an attempt to solve some fundamental problems.
9. I can't be happy until I know the truth.

Now ask them to pair up and fill in the questionnaire on each other's behalf. Discuss the results and discrepancies in a positive, supportive way. What have they learnt? What are the key areas where they could improve their score, and what strategies might they use?

ii) Know it when you hear it
Discuss the following with your team:
- What does curiosity look, sound and feel like from a service person's perspective?
- How will this mindset enhance our customer's experience and add value to our conversation?
- How will curious people approach their day?
- What will be different?
- Role-model being curious by asking them to think about what you can do as a leader to nurture curiosity!

iii) Curiosity top tips
Create cards or post-it notes with the following curiosity tips on them:
- Don't accept face value. Often what we are exposed to is only the tip of the iceberg. Scratch the surface and dive in a little deeper or look at it from a 360-degree perspective, and then investigate any or all the new information that you discover.
- Don't label something as boring. Whenever you label something as boring, you close the door of possibilities. Curious people are unlikely to call something boring. Instead, they see it as a door to an exciting new world. Even if they don't yet have time to explore it, they will leave the door open to be visited another time.
- Ask questions. Be like a little kid or think like a beginner. When we see or read something that peaks our curiosity, we naturally start

thinking 'How' or 'Why'? Asking more questions is like turning over more rocks. You never know what you'll find under there.

- Find a curiosity buddy. Collaboration aids success! It's also more fun when we get curious with someone. It makes for lively discussions and more sharing of ideas. See learning as something fun. If you see learning as a burden, there's no way you will want to dig deeper into anything, which will just make the burden heavier. But, if you think of learning as something fun, you will naturally want to dig deeper. So, look at life through the glasses of fun and excitement and enjoy the learning process.
- Consider 'What If'. Try thinking in three scenarios. Analyse by using the worst, most likely, and best-case scenarios. When aiming for creativity, put your brain into 'Sci-Fi-Mode', asking, what if, in a parallel universe, or what if, in another life time, it had turned out like this?
- Get proactive. It's easy to accept things as they are, but we have to take the initiative if we want to be curious. Being reactive or doing nothing reaps different results to being curious.
- Develop a hungry mind. Back in 1994, George Loewenstein, a professor of Economics and Psychology at Carnegie Mellon University, suggested that curiosity does, in fact, require some initial knowledge. In other words, the more we know, the more we want to know. So, if you're looking to become a bit more curious, you may want to try tapping into some subject matter you don't know much about.
- Be prepared to be wrong. Wanting to always be 'right' stops us from reaching beyond our comfort zone. Take an entrepreneurial attitude and decide to fail better instead!

Ask your team (working in small groups) to discuss the tips and prioritise the top three that would work best for them. Give a bonus prize to someone who is curious and ask if they can come up with their own tips. If no-one does, explain that you had a prize waiting for a curious person!

iv) One mouth, two ears

Set your team a challenge to stop talking and start listening. In their next conversation, ask them to:

- Be more present: recognise that what you're hearing can't possibly be all there is to it.
- Practise acknowledging little details in conversations.
- Focus less on what you're going to say next, and more on the words and information they're choosing to tell you - or not tell you. Listen to understand, not interrupt.
- Discover whether this makes it easier for you to formulate questions, warm up to new perspectives, and learn something new that you may have missed otherwise.

v) Visualise it

Ask your team members to draw a picture representing a 'curious mindset' and how the customer would feel interacting with a person who is curious. This is a very simple one but incredibly effective, as it really makes your team engage with the mindset in a tangible, multi-sensory way. You can replicate this exercise with all the other mindsets.

vi) Think divergently

Give each team member one sheet of paper with 30 small circles on it, and something to draw with. Ask them to turn as many of the blank circles as possible into recognisable objects in three minutes.

Compare results. Look for the quantity of ideas. Ask how many people filled in 10, 15, 20 or more circles? (Most people don't finish.) Next, look for diversity or flexibility in ideas. Are the ideas derivative (a basketball, a baseball, a volleyball) or distinct (a planet, a cookie, a happy face)? If people were drawing their own circles, did anyone 'break the rules' and combine two or more (a snowman or a traffic light)? Were the rules explicit, or just assumed?

MINDSET 3: AGILITY

If you want to get better at anything in life - improve, achieve, be the best you can be - it all starts with the mindset of agility.

The good news is that the very fact you're reading this book already suggests that you'd score pretty highly on a learning agility test. Learning agility is closely linked to that concept of 'growth mindset' we saw in Carol Dweck's experiment at the start of the chapter, and people who have agile mindsets typically do three things.

The first is that they continually seek opportunities to learn. They set new goals, challenge themselves to do things differently, and relish the chance to grow and expand themselves in the process. They're always striving to be themselves, but with that bit more skill added on. The power of this sort of attitude was really brought home to me by a story I was told by my friend's daughter.

A sixth former came into this girl's class - she's eleven - and asked if anyone could sing. My friend's daughter put her hand up and said "I can sing!" The sixth former then invited her along to an audition. Off she went, and it ended up that this little eleven-year-old had accidentally volunteered to do the solo at the start of the sixth form house choir, where she was going to have to sing the first verse of a song in front of the whole school. At this point I stopped her and asked: "Weren't you worried about that in any way?!" Then she said something to me I'll never forget. She said "Do you know what? I've decided that my life at school isn't going to be all about just doing the work. I want to make sure that I get the most out of it. So, I'm going to volunteer for some stuff that I might find quite uncomfortable or get nervous about, but I know that once I've done it, I'll feel really good about it."

So, here's an eleven-year-old who has already worked out, at such a young age, that saying yes to stuff - and yes, worrying about it, but doing it anyway - will give her a real sense of achievement after she's done it. I call that 'life beginning where your comfort zone ends' and, every time I think about agility mindsets, I think about my friend's daughter.

The second thing you notice with people who have very high learning agility is that they don't prickle when they hear feedback. So, these are people who actively seek out feedback, because they know they can learn from it and use it to grow. They even enjoy the process! They find different ways to go out and get feedback from others, but they also continually feedback to themselves. You'll see these people observing themselves in situations, making notes, and tweaking what they're doing based on those notes.

The third sign that someone has a highly agile mindset is that they bounce back quickly from setbacks. They can do this because of the story they tell themselves about what's happened. They reflect on the situation and understand what they can learn to move forward from it - but they don't then worry about it as something that's going to affect them for the rest of their lives. Bounce-back-ability is a tell-tale symptom of someone with a very agile mind; if you think of our most successful business people around today, from Tim Cook to Richard Branson, you'll nearly always find that they've effectively bounced back from a string of setbacks to get where they are today.

The amazing thing about an agile mindset is that it has the ability to turn every challenge into an opportunity, every failure into a step on the path to success. That makes it a seriously powerful tool to have in sales and service, where you face challenges and problems and unpredictable factors every day, simply by the nature of the job.

LEADERSHIP HACKS: AGILITY

i) Learning Council
Create a 'Learning Council'. Find a few people who you trust, tell them something you'd like to improve about yourself, and ask them to hold you accountable. Ask them to feedback on whether they see changes, encourage them to challenge you where necessary - and let them praise you when you do a good job too!

ii) Self-reflection
Deeply reflect on what you really want to change and why you haven't done it already. Talk honestly to yourself about what's holding you back, think through situations when you've managed to succeed against all the odds, and commit yourself to some specific goals and milestones.

iii) Stretch yourself
This is my favourite - encourage yourself to say yes to things you might otherwise have said no to, even if you feel uncomfortable. Remind yourself of my friend's daughter; you know that after it's done you'll feel a huge sense of achievement. It is worth it!

iv) Read
Warren Buffett spends five to six hours per day reading five newspapers and 500 pages of corporate reports. Bill Gates reads fifty books per year. Even though he's the richest man in the world and could afford to hire an army of teachers and consultants, Bill Gates still reads a book a week. In a 2016 New York Times interview, he said, "Reading is still the main way that I both learn new things and test my understanding."[44] Mark Zuckerberg reads at least one book every two weeks. Elon Musk grew up reading two books a day, according to his brother.

As you see some of the most successful people are avid readers. They look to soak up knowledge from wherever they can get it. In today's digital world we are bombarded with online articles, blogs, vlogs and so on. For a mind that is learning agile, it is like being in a candy shop. The trick is carving time out to read and learn. Spend ten minutes each day reading online blogs or a blog linked to the craft of leadership or customer experience.

---

44 https://www.nytimes.com/2016/01/04/fashion/bill-gates-gates-notes-books.html

⚡ CRACK THE CODE: AGILITY

i) How agile are you?

Gather your team together and get them to complete this self-assessment, rating the following statements using a score from 1 to 5, where 1 is 'not like you at all' and 5 is 'very like you'.

1. I seek out new challenges in order to stretch and grow myself.
2. I suspend judgement and remain curious, to better understand a new perspective.
3. I don't accept the status quo.
4. I take responsibility for my learning, i.e. by reading blogs or watching TED talks.
5. I am willing to take the heat if things don't work.
6. I quickly develop new approaches or strategies to address a challenge and/or opportunity.
7. I bounce back quickly from tough situations, treating them as temporary setbacks rather than permanent problems.
8. I seek feedback and input from others to help me better understand a situation.
9. I use lessons learnt from feedback to improve my personal effectiveness.
10. I take time to reflect on and evaluate experiences, drawing practical conclusions and planning what to do as a result.

Now ask them to pair up and fill in the questionnaire on each other's behalf. Discuss the results and discrepancies in a positive, supportive way. What have they learnt? What are the key areas where they could improve their score and what strategies might they use?

ii) Develop bounce-back-ability

When things go wrong for your team, ask them to take a tip from Dan Pink and consider: is this permanent? Have you lost your ability, or were you just having an off day? Is this pervasive? Will all customers be this disruptive or was it just this one? Is this personal? Has performance dipped because you're bad at what you do, or because of market conditions? Encourage them to be realistic and fair and then move forward.

iii) Live brave

Help your team to be brave, challenge the status quo and seek new ways of doing things. 'If You Always Do What You've Always Done, You Always Get What You've Always Gotten.' The only real failure is not taking any action in the first place, so tell them that you will always be open to new ideas, however mad they seem.

MINDSET 4: PRESENCE

Every one of us will have been through a situation in our lives - probably quite regularly - when we're in a conversation with another human being but we feel that we're not being listened to or heard, or that there just isn't a connection going on.

This lack of connection shows up massively in conversations with customers, in any kind of situation, in a number of different ways. One example is where the process of dealing with a query or a sales enquiry is put before the human being that's actually making the request. So, you can find that you're asking questions or stating pieces of information because the process dictates it, rather than really listening to the person in front of you.

Another way it shows up is in what I call the tumbleweed moment. This is where the person that you're dealing with makes some sort of joke as part of the conversation, but it's completely missed because you're so focused on responding to the query, so you get this odd moment where there's an expectation of laughter, but no-one laughs. Awkward.
A third way you see it show up is in missed opportunities to connect. This shows up when a gem or a little piece of gold has been delivered in the conversation - a really human thing to say, like a comment about a child or something emotional about the situation - but it doesn't get picked up on and used in the conversation. You've missed an opportunity to make that human connection because you're not really with the other person.

A final way you see it show up is in more challenging conversations, when someone eventually blurts out "You're just not listening!" That's a sure sign that you're not meeting on the same terms.

The tool we use to help deal with this is called the three circles of presence.[45] It's virtually impossible to teach someone the 'skill of human connection', but it is possible to help them shift their mindset, so I find using these circles the most effective way to help people become more engaged in any conversation.

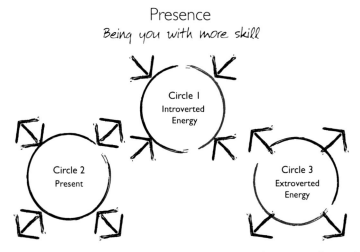

Presence
Being you with more skill

Circle 1
Introverted
Energy

Circle 2
Present

Circle 3
Extroverted
Energy

Withdrawing from a conversation? Feeling a bit threatened? Lacking in confidence? You're in circle 1. You'll also find yourself in circle 1 when you're finding it hard to focus or not paying attention; when your mind is drifting somewhere other than the conversation you're having. We've all been there.

Circle 3 is almost the exact opposite of this. You're in circle three when you find yourself pushing your own agenda over the agenda of the other person - trying to force information through. It's when you're having a conversation with the attitude 'It's my way or the highway, mate', with elements of control and domination in play (and not in a fun way).

---

45 Based on the work by Patsy Rodenburg – 'circles of energy' published in her excellent book 'Presence'. Recommended reading – 'Presence: How to Use Positive Energy for Success in Every Situation 28 May 2009 - Patsy Rodenburg

It doesn't have to be aggressive, however; it shows up whenever you're putting the process before the person, even if that's happening in quite a subtle way. When you're on the receiving end of circle 3, it feels like someone is talking 'past' you, which is where the 'hey! are you listening to me?' moment comes in.

In between these extremes, we find the lovely circle 2: the circle of presence. This is the circle where we're listening, we're engaged, we're connecting, we're noticing what's happening in the conversation, we're responding to the other person's agenda, and we're adapting and being flexible so that we end up with a win-win. In this circle, you'll find yourself asking questions and really trying to tune into what's being said - and trying to tune into what's being meant, too. It's a very equal and human place to be.

What I love about the three circles of presence is their simplicity. They put actually quite complex psychological states into language even a child could understand. I even use them with my kids, in fact. But more on that later.

When it comes to practising the art of being present, it comes down to choice. Frustrating as it might sound, there aren't specific skills you can learn or things you can do other than trying to consciously enter conversations every time. As you go into a conversation, get into the habit of asking yourself: is my mind focused on this conversation? Am I fully present and connected? Is my mind in this? My spirit? My heart?

 # LEADERSHIP HACKS: PRESENCE

i) Your circle

As leaders, we need to be present and raise our heads and notice what's going on for our people and how they are performing, so we are best positioned to support their growth. Consider the last time you spent a day with your team and ask yourself the following questions:

- Were all of your team present for their shift?
- Who had an amazing day?
- What type of day did each individual have?

- What types of customer conversations did your team have?
- What buzz was generated by your team and in the whole office?
- Who had the best customer conversation in your team yesterday?
- How many genuine smiles did you spot throughout the day?
- When did you notice people doing great things for others?

It's amazing what we can miss when we're not present.

ii) Turn up the dial
You don't have to experience a spiritual epiphany or inner transformation to become present. By making small changes you can have a big impact on the way you think, which will manifest in how you behave. It is about focusing on moments – achieving a state of presence in conversations that matter, whether they're difficult conversations at work or with your spouse at home.

Give yourself daily challenges that force you to slow down and notice what's going on around you. Practise at home; turn up the dial on your 'presence' by 10 per cent and see the difference it makes to your relationships. It is not easy, but through conscious awareness and effort you can reap huge benefits.

CRACK THE CODE: PRESENCE

i) How present are you?
Gather your team together and get them to complete this self-assessment, rating the following statements using a score from 1 to 5, where 1 is 'not like you at all' and 5 is 'very like you'.

1. I don't get easily distracted.
2. I take notes of key words and data when I am talking to a colleague or customer.
3. I take time to understand without making assumptions.
4. I always let someone finish speaking and never interrupt.
5. I can keep an open mind even if I don't always agree.
6. I never multitask when speaking to someone on the phone.

7. I notice little things about other people.
8. I regularly check my understanding in conversations and in meetings.
9. I am conscious of my body language and the importance of acknowledging presence through both physical and verbal signs.

Now ask them to pair up and fill in the questionnaire on each other's behalf. Discuss the results and discrepancies in a positive, supportive way. What have they learnt? What are the key areas where they could improve their score, and what strategies might they use?

ii) Thinking in circles
Working in small groups, ask your team to consider the following questions in terms of how they interact with customers:
• What situations put you in circle 1? What is the impact on your customer and you?
• What situations put you in circle 3? What is the impact on your customer and you?
• What are the benefits of being in circle 2 for you and your customer?

iii) Press delete
Challenge your team to think about the assumptions, biases and moods they might be working from when they deal with customers. Encourage them to try to mentally 'clear their history' before every conversation so they can be truly present.

MINDSET 5: IMAGINATION

According to research from Dr Fred Luskin of Stanford University, we each have 60,000 thoughts in a single day - and 90 per cent of them are the same as the ones we had yesterday.[46]

Just think about that for a second. It never fails to blow my mind. We are all effectively sleepwalking through life. And inevitably, if you're working in a job that involves a lot of repetition, you are going to end up sleepwalking through a lot of your conversations with customers. The more routine you have, the more habit you create; and the more habit you create, the more you end up applying memory to the situation. So, whatever you've done before, you apply to the situation going on right now. We call it working from memory, not imagination.

Unsurprisingly, working from memory can have a big negative impact in service and sales. If you're on autopilot or operating out of habit, you can often end up with the wrong solution for the right question. You can end up giving the customer an experience where they're not really being heard. Or you can end up with a situation where the customer's half way through a sentence but you've already worked out in your own mind what you think the answer is, so you're effectively answering things before the conversation has even started.

Thankfully, there's a piece of evolutionary science that can help us here. Humans are born with something called divergent thinking programmed into our brains. We're geniuses at it by the age of five. The standard test used to measure divergent thinking is to give someone a paperclip and ask them to come up with the most possible uses they can think of for it.

Grab a paperclip. Try it now.

46 https://www.forbes.com/sites/christinecomaford/2012/04/04/got-inner-peace-5-ways-to-get-it-now/#69763cd66727

How many uses did you find? Fifteen? Ten? Twenty? Five-year-olds tend to come up with closer to two hundred, because they're entirely unbothered about what convention and experience tells us is a 'normal' or practical use for a paperclip. Sadly, researchers find that as we go through life, our ability to practise divergent thinking steeply declines. A longitudinal study of kindergarten children measured 98 per cent of them at genius level in divergent thinking. Five years later, when they were aged eight to ten years, those at genius level had dropped to 50 per cent. After another five years, the number of divergent thinking geniuses had fallen further still.[47]

The great educationalist Sir Ken Robinson believes that we are "educating people out of their creativity",[48] training them to come up with a single right answer, not many possible ones. A lot of research has been done into why we lose this imaginative power. But whatever the reason, the important thing is that we find ways to wake ourselves up from this mental sleepwalking, and come to customer conversations with a mindset of multiple possibilities.

Doing what's right for the customer means working with what's happening in the conversation in the moment, but also applying just a little bit of imagination too, allowing just a bit of our five-year-old selves to join in. Is there more than one possibility for this conversation? What other options might there be? If we're listening closely to the customer, we can use their words as triggers to set off a whole range of potential ideas.

Every customer conversation should involve a quick check: am I working from a place of imagination or a place of memory? If you just keep asking yourself that every day, your imagination muscle wakes up and you start to find more and more possibilities with each conversation. It also helps to make space in your day to think, really think about new ideas to solve the work challenges that you face. And use your colleagues, too; this happens all too rarely, but if you're working with a group of people to achieve the same aim, use them shamelessly!

47 ps://www.ncbi.nlm.nih.gov/pmc/articles/PMC3184540/
48 https://www.ted.com/talks/ken_robinson_says_schools_kill_creativity

Ask them every so often what they find works well and you'll discover a whole new lot of ideas and insights to keep your own conversations fresh.

IRL: CHILD'S PLAY

If you've ever been to Disneyworld, you might have witnessed some imaginative mindsets in action. Disney encourages its staff to respond creatively to the most simple customer enquiry.

So, if you approach a helper to ask what time the next show starts, rather than automatically replying "Three pm", they've been trained to think about the particular context of the moment and come up with a different answer every time.

"Well, it starts at three, but seeing as it's now two forty-five, I'd head over now to make sure you get a good seat. It's pretty busy today, so I wouldn't take any chances, and they sell snacks there if you want to get settled in."

LEADERSHIP HACKS: IMAGINATION

i) Daydream believer
You might have been told off for daydreaming at school, but it's one of the most powerful human tools we have. Try to build a few minutes of daydreaming into your day, letting the images and experiences of the past few hours wash through your mind and combine in unexpected ways. I like to do this when I make myself a coffee in the early afternoon.

ii) Leave something undone
If at the end of the day you leave a task slightly unfinished, it may be easier to start on the next day. That's because cognitive threads are left hanging in your mind - as you go about your non-work activities, your subconscious might hook onto them and give you a sudden insight.

iii) Engage with people who are different from you

We hang out with people who are like us, and while doing so may be comforting, it's not stretching. Also, try imagining yourself as someone else such as someone in finance, a customer or one of your team members. How would they see the world?

iv) Make ideas compete against each other

Select two ideas and define how they're different, even in the most subtle ways. Or if you have more than ten ideas, write each one on a sticky note. Move ideas that seem related close together; you'll arrive at idea clusters and can look at interesting differences between ideas.

v) Wake up your right brain.

The right brain is your imagination centre. Because the right brain hemisphere controls the left side of your body, you can activate your imagination by breathing out of only your left nostril, jumping up and down on your left foot, and writing with your left hand. You can also wake up the right side of the brain by doing something artistic such as drawing or playing a musical instrument.

vi) Disrupt your habits

Take a different route to work, try food you've never eaten before, listen to a music genre you normally don't listen to, read different magazines. Explore something new and try something you've always wondered about. Boxing, anyone?

⚡ CRACK THE CODE: IMAGINATION

i) Why can't a chair be a raft?

Developed by J.P. Guilford in 1967, the Alternative Uses Test[49] stretches your creativity by giving you two minutes to think of as many uses as possible for an everyday object like a chair, coffee mug or brick. Set this task for your team in your next meeting. You could even make it a regular part of a weekly meeting, using a different object every time.

---

49 Guilford, J.P., Christensen, P.R., Merrifield, P.R., and Wilson, R.C., 1960. Alternative Uses Manual. Sheri-

ii) From memory to imagination

Play this Ken Robinson video to your team to introduce the concept of divergent thinking: https://www.youtube.com/watch?v=hzBa-frc2JA. Explain to them that the idea is to use their imagination to tailor your service for your customer. Rather than trotting out the same standard answer to every customer, every time they get asked the same question, make it more meaningful and personal. It's about creating 'small moments of wonder'.

Then ask them to work in pairs and list the top ten questions they get asked by customers in your job. What is the standard answer they usually give, from their memory? What answer could they give if they were being more creative and imaginative? What impact might this have on their customer conversation?

Ask them to use their new answers when they next get asked the question... while also personalising it to suit their customer. Debrief at the end of the day, to see what worked well and what did not land so well.

 CRUNCH TIME: TEST YOUR MINDSETS

So, it's time to take a good hard look at how you're doing. How are those mindsets shaping up? Gather your people together and start by asking: What are the key collective mindsets we are aiming for? Then split the group into three small teams. Give each team one of the mindsets and ask them to discuss and present back on:

- What is this mindset all about?
- What would be different around here internally if everyone embraced the mindset?
- What would be different for customers if everyone embraced that mindset?

Allow some prep time then ask each group to present back. Share findings, discuss as a wider group and fill in any blanks your people may have. Next, collectively discuss:

- What results would you like to be achieving six months from now? (Flip chart the responses)
- How can X mindset help us achieve that?
- What action do we need to take as a team next, linked to our vision and the five key mindsets?

Flip chart agreed actions and develop a team action plan, with actions for you as the leader and individual actions for team members. Remind your team to be accountable! Share your personal commitments to achieving the vision and ask each team member to do the same. Revisit this vision and the commitments at future team meetings.

So, are you and your teams starting to feel as flexible as a four-year-old, as imaginative as a five-year-old, and as brave as an eleven-year-old doing a solo in front of the whole school?

If the answer is yes, or at least 'we're on the right track', you can move onto Chapter 7 - and get up close and personal with Voldemort.

>_ SOURCE CODE: CHAPTER 6

There are seven crucial behaviours that help create great customer conversations, but these simply will not stick if you fail to show up to conversations in the right way.

Our mindset creates a lens through which we look at the world and determines how we behave. There are five mindsets that are key to cracking the conversation code:

1. Accountability: arguably the most important mindset, this involves taking full ownership of your life and work. The process is not always easy, but the accountability ladder can help visualise and shift accountability for both leaders and teams.
2. Curiosity: when you're genuinely curious, you assume that other people may have information that you do not. You also assume that others may see things that you may miss. As a result, you're able to uncover powerful and unexpected issues and ideas.
3. Agility: agile people know that we are all just works in progress and see learning as the fuel that keeps us growing. They're not just open to change; they seek it out.
4. Presence: we know it when we feel it... and when we don't. When you are not present, people can tell. When you are, people respond. When you're in circle 2 of presence, you're fully attuned to the other person, and bring it out in them.
5. Imagination: working from imagination rather than memory allows you to create the best possible outcome for whoever you're with, here and now. Using a little bit of imagination will help you break beyond self-imposed boundaries to do the right thing.

CHAPTER 7: UNCOACHING

CALLING TIME ON VOLDEMORT

While working on a project for a large telco firm a couple of years ago, my colleague Steve had the opportunity to spend some time with the people on an impressively high-performing sales and service site. These guys were the real deal: happy to be there, engaged, productive, effective. They really did put the customer first, and they were delivering the results to prove it.

But as Steve got to know them, it turned out that their story had an interesting twist.

Four years ago, this super-site had in fact been the worst performing site in the business. And yet the people there now - the ones winning all the awards - were in large part exactly the same people that had been there four years before. So, what changed?

Voldemort.

Four years ago, the leader at the time was, shall we say, "not spoken of highly". People in the business didn't even like to use his name - hence the nickname Voldemort. Thankfully, he had now been replaced by a brilliant new woman - let's call her Debbie - who embodied the ethos of supportive, positive, people-focused growth. Debbie shared stories about what the business stood for every week, in a way that people could get on board with, and that approach had trickled down to her managers, who had clearly become excellent at coaching their teams.

But the second twist in this tale came when Steve witnessed some of those managers coaching in action, and gave them feedback on what a great job they had done. Normally, when you give this sort of feedback, full of specific examples of how they nailed it, the coach is delighted. With these managers, the reaction was shock and, more than once, tears. The feedback contrasted so strongly with their own view of themselves that they just couldn't reconcile their terrible self-image with Steve's heartfelt praise.

The sad truth was that Voldemort's leadership style had left deep scars. Under Debbie's guidance and with some support from Steve, those scars were healing, and the confidence was definitely returning. But it was an important reminder that bad leadership can wreck more than people's career prospects. It can damage their lives.

To push the Voldemort analogy - Harry Potter bore the scars after an attack on his parents, and he was never going to amount to much under the hostile guidance of Mr Dursley. But under Dumbledore, he became the greatest wizard of all time. Our telco managers were the same - they bore the scars, they were brought up in a hostile environment, but under the guidance of a supreme talent, they became true coaching wizards.

Unfortunately, this was not the first time Steve had experienced leaders who - mostly unwittingly, and often maybe even well intentioned - have destroyed people's confidence and negatively affected their personal lives, all the while being utterly blind to the impact of their behaviour. However, it was the moment when he decided to start becoming much more vocal in the industry about the power that managers at all levels wield, and how cautious we must be as leaders with people and their lives.

That's why I asked Steve to write this chapter. His passion, vision and expertise have shaped our approach to 'uncoaching' at Blue Sky, which has been a huge part of our success. Let me assure you: you're in the safest of hands for the next few pages. So... over to Steve.

IRL: HUMAN FALLOUT

During Sally's interview with Bob Chapman, he talked about his motivation for creating the Truly Human Leadership approach, and what he said has stayed with me ever since.

"The one thing that comes back is that the way we lead in business - I was never taught this - I never heard it - the way we treat people when we organise businesses affects the way these people go home and treat their spouses and raise their children," he said.

"When we look at the broken-ness of society today, the frustration around the world - when you realise that 88 per cent of all people feel that they work for an organisation that does not care about them and the way that makes them feel about themselves when they go home, when they feel used and unappreciated and we expect them to go home and be a good spouse and to be a good parent when they're treated forty hours a week with no respect and dignity....

"A New York Times columnist made the following statement: 'While we do good in the world, could we do less harm?' All of you who write cheques for good causes - how did you get your money? Was it by abusing and using other people or was it by doing good things? While we try to do good in the world, do we realise how much harm we are doing? Another statistic - 74 per cent of all illnesses are chronic – the biggest cause of chronic illness is stress and the biggest cause of stress is work. In America, there is a 20 per cent increase in heart attacks on Monday mornings – so when we look at children today and say 'Gee, children of today aren't what they used to be', they are the product of marriages that we have helped destroy.

Ninety per cent of the feedback that we get on our leadership model is how it affects their parenting and their marriage."

THE C-WORD

Coaching has a horrible reputation. I should know. I am one. There's a vast industry out there, with everything from books to conferences to blogs to online courses promising to turn you into a "master coach." Which is all well and good, if you have money and time to burn. But for your average newly-minted manager, with barely twenty years of life experience and an inbox larger than their one-bedroom flat, becoming a 'master coach' is a distant dream - not to mention entirely unnecessary.

The one thing we don't need in the business world is more 'managers', with a big aggressive M. This world needs fewer scorers, processors feedbackers, demanders, command and controllers, critiquers, short-term thinkers and empire-building protectionists. What it needs are more experts - experts who can engage, motivate, energise, praise, thank, and generally turn the lowest performing team in a business into the highest performing team in a business.

What we do need is a whole phalanx of people who are brilliant at encouraging, stimulating, invigorating, tickling, inspiring and otherwise nudging their people to keep making it human every day, in small and concrete ways. It is this stuff that turns the dial, that shifts the needle, and that delivers an ROI. It's this stuff that helps create a lasting culture where people want to show up, are happy, engaged, productive and effective. And it costs nothing, only time.

I call it uncoaching. I'm being purposefully provocative. Let me explain.

If you google 'sport stacking', you'll come across some videos of people stacking cups, fast. Really, really fast. The current world record holder is an eighteen-year-old American kid called William Orrell, who can stack a 'cycle' of cups in 4.8 seconds. Go online now and watch him do it. It's extraordinary.

When I show a room of people a video of William stacking cups and then ask them "Put your hand up if you think you can do this", they all keep their hands firmly under the table and look at me as if I'm mad. So, then I ask them to nominate a coach. I show the coach the video and give them the cups and, time and time and time again, the coach will have a bloody good go at trying to coach this person on how to do it… with absolutely zero knowledge on how to actually stack cups. There's something about being called a 'coach' that makes people think, if they just cheerlead hard enough and make a few random suggestions, they can help someone else do anything. Even something as mad-hard as speed-stacking cups.

The world is full of coaches like that. And actually, the cheerleader approach often works fine for life coaching, when the answer lies within the person being coached and they just need a bit of help, a few smart questions, to root it out. But customer experience is - brace yourself - a skill. If you don't know how to do it - and we're talking science-backed behaviours and mindsets here - you will not somehow magically find the answer within yourself.

If you understand the building blocks of how to stack cups - and there are specific building blocks, specific steps in process - then you can very easily coach someone on how to do it. But you've also got to know what good looks like (in this case, William Orrell). The same goes for customer experience. If you're to coach it effectively, you absolutely have to know what brilliant customer experience looks and sounds and feels like and, if you don't, you haven't got a cat in hell's chance of coaching someone else.

So you don't need to go on a magical 'coaching' training course but you do need to have rock-solid skills in how to deliver great customer sales and service. I remember, about twenty years ago, someone in the industry publishing a book with the central message that "managers don't need to be experts in how to do the work, they just need to be good people leaders". It made my blood boil. You simply cannot coach skill without being an expert in the skill. If you're going to hire a tennis coach, you're going to hire someone who can play tennis.

In my experience, organisations are full of coaches who are very well trained technically but whose emphasis is entirely on asking open questions, with a view to helping the individual to find the answer within themselves. The thing is if you don't know how to do the skill, you're just not going to find it within you. Someone has to help.

So you don't need an organisation full of noisy self-proclaimed coaches who can help people 'find it within themselves'. You need an organisation full of underground 'tempered radicals' - we call them uncoaches - who know what good looks like and can get those behaviours to show up time and again in other people. For that, you need all the knowledge Sally has already imparted in this book, the dedication to follow it through with the exercises… and then a host of little techniques that require minimal skill but a lot of imagination and energy.

So, unlike the previous chapters, what I lay out here isn't a process best followed step by cumulative step. It's a deluge of ideas; a feast of tactics you can try to keep real actions showing up. Suck them and see. Test a new one every day. Add your own. I've chosen the ones below because they've worked particularly well for certain clients over the years, but that doesn't mean they're best for you. We're always chopping, changing, adding, testing and updating ours. The most important thing is to keep trying. Keep doing. Never stop.

I've split them into three sections: stuff it helps to understand first (concepts), things you can try doing (methods) and different ways you can try doing them (techniques).

CONCEPTS: FEEDING THE PIG

Let's start with a brief story. Over the years, a plethora of metrics have arisen to measure performance. Many sayings have grown up around them like 'If you don't measure it, you can't manage it'. Sound familiar?

I was in a call centre recently, coaching side by side with an advisor when, out of the blue, I heard, "Get yourself out of wrap…your call length is too high". A confused look followed from both me and the advisor. I noticed that there were 25 calls in the queue and the number of calls answered in twenty seconds or less - a key metric - had hit 48 per cent. I could sense the stress of the manager and their desire to get the calls answered as quickly as possible.

The manager continued, "Your call handling time has been high all week. I need you to get it down and quickly." The manager promptly walked off to tear a piece out of the next person in an adjacent team.

I turned to the advisor and asked, "How are you going to get the call length down?"

They looked back at me, hoping I would give them the answer. After a pause they said, "I don't know".

Therein lies the problem. Putting to one side the nature of the feedback and how it was delivered, which in itself was not great, the manager was telling his people 'what' to do… but not 'how' to do it. The manager was transfixed by the number, the output, rather than the input needed to drive the number up. What the person needed was some coaching and support around how to signpost better in the conversation and ask better questions. Both of these behaviours would have helped reduce the amount of time they spent on the call and increased customer satisfaction.

I call this 'weighing the pig'.

Let me explain. There's an old fable about a farmer who has a prize pig. He has to get this pig to an exact weight to be able to sell it at the optimum price. Each day this farmer takes the pig down to the market to weigh it. Every day, he discovers that the pig isn't yet fat enough, so he returns to the farm (a three-hour round trip). He does this for weeks, trudging back and forth, hoping something will change. At no point, does he step back and actually ask: how am I going to make this pig weigh more? How am I going to better feed this pig?

So how do we feed the pig in customer experience? By uplifting, nurturing and human coaching and support. By fighting your negativity bias and sharing positive stories, you've already learnt powerful ways to build a climate that will feed people every day. So, when the pressure to hit targets gets tougher and tougher, don't make the mistake of cutting back on the good stuff and doubling the stress.

Don't weigh the pig. Feed the pig.

EYES UP

When I start working with a new client, I always like to walk through their workspace several times throughout my first day. My mission is to notice how managers and leaders are talking and working shoulder to shoulder with their people, and how many are 'PC warriors' nailed to their chairs and glued to their screens. If there are no more than two managers out of ten in any given walkabout out of their chairs, then I estimate the amount of time being dedicated to their people as less than 20 per cent. It's a crude, simple measurement, but it doesn't half get the measure of an organisation more quickly and efficiently than some 150-page diagnostic report.

Twenty per cent isn't rare. Almost without exception, all of the businesses I have worked in suffer from an epidemic of people who are glued to their screens, reading emails, trawling through data, producing reports, just "dealing with stuff". While it may feel harsh to call this type of behaviour negligent or wilful, is it too much of a jump to call it neglect?

This is not the fault of the managers. As we saw in Chapter 3, it is up to the leadership team to clear the path. And 'eyes down', as I like to call it, is usually unconscious, not wilful. But that's exactly the problem - it often passes by unnoticed and the people with their eyes down just don't understand its toxic impact. This links into so many concepts we've already visited in this book so far: sleepwalking through life, failing to be in circle 2, lacking curiosity for what's going on right now. In an uncoaching context, it can mean failing to notice the great work someone has done, or failing to see danger signs that your teams need more help to thrive.

The likely next step on this slippery slope is wilful blindness. Having unconsciously let things slip, more serious situations start to arise that do finally force their way into your consciousness. Perhaps those mini tantrums from the guy whose behaviour is difficult to manage slowly increase in frequency. Perhaps the performance of that inconsistent woman starts to trend more towards the consistently bad. Poor timekeeping, process-driven customer conversations, negativity about the latest product launch… these are all signs that your climate is moving in the wrong direction. But you just don't have the time or energy to deal with it right now.

This always reminds me of taking your kids out to a restaurant when they're in a naughty mood. They're playing up, they're throwing rolls, they're making snarky comments. They know they're being naughty. You know they're being naughty. Everyone in the restaurant knows they're being naughty. But sometimes you choose to be wilfully blind because you're tired, you're desperate to have a good time and you know that a confrontation might make things worse. And by you, I mean me! I've been that parent more than once.

The final stop on this journey is social loafing. This is a concept from social psychology, and it can be summarised as: "Well, if that person can get away with it, then I should be able to do it as well." Research finds that people in groups exert less effort than when they are working alone; in other words, when a climate gets toxic enough, we drag ourselves down to the lowest common denominator. It's the old 'broken windows' theory in action again - but going in the wrong direction.

If you know about these three steps, you can start to understand why a manager who began by simply spending too much time absorbed in reports on her screen might almost imperceptibly start to morph into a Voldemort. And the crucial thing here is: it's your job to stop it from happening, both by clearing the path and helping your managers stay present.

The way to do this is very, very simple.

Visualise a floor of eight front line managers. What would happen if, every morning, they lived and breathed the mantra "Eyes up: turn on your people before turning on your PC"?

Imagine them, all eight of them, on their feet: welcoming people, helping them get logged in, asking how they are, dealing with any issues, engaging in a bit of banter, talking passionately about your ethos, sharing positive stories from the week so far and, very importantly, discussing a specific behaviour or mindset to focus on that day. This activity could take as little as 15 minutes, but the key thing is that it sets up the first magic minutes of the team's day.

I don't need to spell out all the positive impacts of what's happening in this exercise, but I do want to point out the way it employs a brain effect known as priming. In psychology, priming involves activating particular representations or associations in someone's memory just before carrying out an action or task. There are over 40 years of research to prove its efficacy. Derren Brown uses it to do many of his tricks. It explains why, in one research experiment,[50] people who had been exposed to words about old age walked out of the building slower than they walked in. Or why, when you buy a new car, you suddenly see a lot more of those cars.

I'm not saying you try to do some sort of Svengali brainwashing technique here; only that you simply and explicitly remind your people that the customer is their priority, and remind them of the behaviours and mindsets that will make that a reality. It's a simple, powerful tool that is easy to use. Every day. Think of it as 'switching your people on.'

And if your managers are sharing those positive stories about the company every morning and role-modelling the right behaviours, something very cool starts to happen: community policing.[51] The need for a top-down Voldemort to monitor, control and catch people out starts to disappear as the workforce themselves hold each other accountable in a much more positive and constructive way.

Parenting is a good analogy here once again. As parents, it's all too easy to spend most of our time telling our kids what they shouldn't do (play up in a restaurant) or what they shouldn't be (rowdy, thoughtless). However, I know that my words have more effect, and I always feel

50 Bargh, J. A., Chen, M., & Burrows, L. (1996). Automaticity of social behavior: Direct effects of trait construct and stereotype activation on action. Journal of Personality and Social Psychology, 71, 230.
51 https://www.amazon.co.uk/Ultimate-Question-Revised-Expanded-Customer-Driven/dp/1422173356

better about them, when I (occasionally) remember to create a vision of the behaviour that we do want (be polite and grateful) rather than call out the negative behaviour that we don't.

When you have a shared vision for how you are as a team, how you treat each other and how you talk to customers, community policing kicks in. The spiral starts to go up, rather than down. And 'eyes up' isn't just for the morning - it must be reiterated throughout the day.

Who looks like they could do with an uncoaching intervention? Who has just thrown their headset down? Who's very quiet and not interacting with the team? Who's being vocally negative and draining the team? Who looks like a 'mood hoover' just stopped by their desk?

Even in highly pressured environments, leaders must timetable and protect the time for managers to continually help their people tune back in. It's presence mindset in action. It's simple, it's free, it's fast and it's effective. Why the hell wouldn't you?

SMALL CHANGE, BIG DIFFERENCE

I love the proverb from the Dalai Lama "If you think you're too small to make a difference, try sleeping with a mosquito in the room". Hopefully, at this point in our journey, you'll have already learnt that you only need to make a small change to make a big difference. The 'eyes up' exercise above is one of the simplest demonstrations of that.

A more dramatic example is the Share My Dabba initiative. With 200,000 children going hungry on the streets of Mumbai every day, the dabbawallas who deliver lunch to people throughout the city were given 'Share My Dabba' stickers to hand out with their pails so that customers could mark the unfinished food they wanted to share. The dabbawallas then set aside the stickered pails and volunteers redistribute them to hungry children. All it takes is a sticker - but the impact is huge.

So, remember, when it comes to uncoaching, don't make it difficult. Make it easy. From doing the long walk, ditching an unnecessary weekly meeting to tweaking one word in a routine customer question, become expert at spotting the small things that will make a big difference - and encourage your people to do the same.

How much pressure do you put on yourself as a coach to drive an impact in every conversation? How much pressure do you put on your team of coaches to deliver? How much pressure do you think those coaches feel to drive a difference every time? We still see so much protectionism in business about the effectiveness of coaching. Leaders obsess over documenting sessions and insist that managers spend precious time trying to tie interventions directly to results. But we all know deep down that human development simply doesn't work like that.

Instead, how liberating would it be to accept that, if you're a good uncoach, two in ten of your sessions will drive a positive behavioural change? That if you're a really great one that number may soar... to three?! Explicitly stating that you don't expect every positive behaviour change to drive an improved hard result will, ironically, make it much easier for effective uncoaching to flourish, and for both staff and customers to experience the uplift.

So, try having a conversation with your people, in your own words, but that sounds something like this: "Just uncoach. Just do it. Don't stress out. You won't shift behaviour immediately, or certainly not get a result on ten coaching sessions out of ten. If you show people you are interested, and if you get stuck in, stuff will happen. Just a little bit of stuff. But making a little bit of stuff happen every single day, will probably make you manager of the year! So, go for it. Engage your people, listen to them, observe them, talk openly about what you have observed and, critically…only ever ask them to change one small thing that you both think might make a difference."

Removing the pressure from coaching and adopting a positive, effortless uncoaching approach really can transform it from a stressful task everyone hates and mistrusts into the secret engine behind your organisation's award-winning customer climate.

IRL: THE BRILLIANT FAILURE

We ran a service culture change programme in a large FTSE 100 business, focusing the front line uncoaching on ten key behaviours. Three-quarters of the way through Phase One of the programme, having covered around 1100 frontline service people, our client embarked on some large-sample call listening activity in order to see the change in the behaviours. The feedback was far from favourable.

"We are not seeing very much uplift in the behaviours at all. In fact we're barely seeing 60 per cent of them show up. The only significant change is in two behaviours and even that isn't as much as we would like, while some sporadic uplift in another two behaviours seems to be department and site dependent."

For sure, this was a difficult conversation to field from a client who was normally very much on board with our approach. This project was an abject failure - right?

Wrong. The good news is that at that particular moment the service metric was turning, and there was even an uplift in the revenue driven by the service teams. And to compound the success, there was a huge discrepancy not just against the baseline, but also against those sites that had been trained. Oh, and staff engagement scores across the trained sites also showed a significant uplift compared to both the baseline and other sites.

So, what was going on?

This programme was living proof of small change, big difference. Even though not all the behaviours had changed, the ones that had, really made an impact. They were ones that made sense to the front line, were the ones that were most powerful in terms of the customer's experience.

So, if we'd only focused on what was going wrong with our strategy, we'd have missed all the stuff that was going right. The learning here was that doing less got a better result.

Once you start uncoaching in this way, the rule of marginal gains kicks in, as the number of touchpoints soars. Take the 'eyes up' example. If each manager, team leader or coach manages to 'wake up' one person on their team of twelve, and remind two more people of the focus for that day through priming, that's three positive changes from just one uncoaching intervention.

Will this measurably drive a shift in the individual's or team's performance that day? It's literally impossible to tell. But the cumulative effect of those changes over each week and month should start to register in one simple way: "How does it FEEL around here?" "Oh, yeah…better." That's all. But that's a hell of a lot. You've just become the world's most efficient climate change scientist.

Which segues beautifully into our next concept.

RETURN ON ENERGY

Many managers (and team members) dread coaching sessions because they take up precious time they could be using to do some "actual work". But a conversation that makes a tangible difference to performance doesn't have to take an hour. In fact, the likelihood of having a good return on the effort expended is likely to decrease the longer the session takes. So, the best uncoaching sessions are usually the shortest, because they have a much higher ROE, or return on the energy that's been given to it - by both parties.

But ROE isn't just improved by keeping an eye on time. It's also essential to remember that the past doesn't matter, and to bring every uncoaching intervention 'back to the future'. Too often coaching involves looking back at a previous customer conversation and focusing on what needed to be done back then. Unless you have a DeLorean with a flux capacitor to go back in time, that's as pointless as wishing you'd married the girl you kissed at the school disco when you were fifteen. What matters is what you're going to do tomorrow, and how you're going to make a real-life customer conversation more successful when it counts.

Let's use an example to bring both of these ROE concepts to life.

Some observations of Paul, our sales person, reveal that he needs help with a certain behaviour. It's not helping sales and it may even be a bit questionable from a service point of view. Traditionally, this could mean a twenty-minute critical feedback session, or worse: a forty-five minute non-directive 'pull coaching' session to get Paul to realise that "behaviour Y is better than behaviour X" and/or that "'we should never do X as it's a bit dodgy.'"

On a good day, when he's reasonably high up the accountability ladder, Paul might adopt a 'must try harder' attitude and make an effort to swap behaviour X for behaviour Y.

On a bad day, Paul may well have a reaction to the feedback which would actually drive his performance down! There is a very real risk of spending forty-five minutes of two people's precious time and getting a worse result. It's an ROE travesty!

So, what might an ROE-savvy uncoach do instead?

One of my favourite techniques is the SWAT team. To do this you'd take three sales people (including Paul) to one side first thing in the morning, and share the critical information that behaviour Y seems to have good results in the other team, and that a lack of it is correlated with poor performance. You'd then finish up this brief chat with something along the lines of: "Could the three of you give an extra push and focus on behaviour Y for the rest of the day, and we'll break early at the end of the day for a cuppa and a quick debrief to how it's gone?"

What just happened, in your five-minute chat? Let's pick it apart. First, you focused Paul on what you want him to do, in a way that avoided making it personal. Then, you only focused on the positive behaviour you want to show up (Y), not the one you want to ditch (X). You also injected a subtle bit of competition to make the behaviour more emotionally compelling. And you not only harnessed the power of the magic minute, by starting the day off with an energising call to action - you set it up for a peak ending, with your cuppa and quick debrief. Plus, you engaged three people with this uplifting micro-session, rather than just one.

How's that for ROE?

Remember: it doesn't take hours to drive performance; it takes minutes. The SWAT team example is just one of many ROE-rich techniques. So, get creative, and think about how you can pack as much ROE as possible into any uncoaching you might do.

METHODS: WALK AND TALK

Every conversation you have is an opportunity to uncoach in some way. So, whenever you're walking with one of your team, start a conversation and use it as a stealth opportunity to uncoach.

This not only saves time but encourages vulnerability and creativity. Most of us know this from our personal lives - it's much easier to be honest with your partner when you're strolling side by side than when you're eyeballing each other across a table. And the best ideas tend to emerge during a country ramble, not when you're stuck behind your desk.

Even if you don't have a specific issue you want to work on with someone, get into the habit of grabbing opportunities to 'walk and talk' just for the hell of it. If your offices have outside space, use it. You never know what you might learn. Even if you get wet.

PEER TO PEER

It's kind of crazy how easy it is to forget that one of the biggest tools you have in your uncoaching box is the people around you. Everyone in your team is great at something, and that something will be different for everyone, so helping people to learn from each other immeasurably increases your team's collective expertise. This also liberates you from the need to know everything your people need to learn, because *someone* in your team will always be able to fill in your weak spots.

One of our clients, a global TV and broadband provider, called peer to peer the "most beneficial thing you have shown us in this whole awesome programme". They reported that "scheduling P2P moving forward was at least **a**, maybe even **the**, critical factor in not only sustaining but continuing to grow the sales performance in our inbound sales team".

This method really puts the 'un' in uncoaching, because it involves you stepping back and become more of a curator than a coach. It's a totally different mindset to the usual coaching culture, and embeds uncoaching right at the heart of your climate. It also builds upon lots of the behaviours we've covered so far, by breaking down barriers, encouraging more sharing of positive stories, and embedding more accountability (if you've just uncoached someone on a particular behaviour, you'd better bloody make sure you're doing it yourself!)

Of course, peer to peer might sound risky if you've inherited (or created) a dysfunctional, underperforming, cynical team. You might want to wait until you've had a couple of months to build that permission climate before you give it a go. Start by floating the idea at a team meeting and then support people who are willing to give it a try. Ask them to pair up, listen in to each other's conversations and give each other positive feedback. Make sure you have already demonstrated what good looks like and shared these concepts and techniques.

And don't forget to be the first to walk your own talk. Ask one of your own peers to come and observe you uncoaching, and then give you some feedback. It might sound scary but think of what Sally's friend's eleven-year-old daughter would say - life starts where your comfort zone ends.

THE POWER OF PRAISE

A Gallup study found that 67 per cent of employees who strongly agree that their manager focuses on their strengths or positive characteristics are engaged, compared with just 31 per cent of employees who strongly agree that their manager focuses on their weaknesses[52] . In other words, praise isn't just fuzzy-wuzzy feel-good - it's hard-numbers effective.

But why is it so powerful? When Sally talked to Simon Sinek last year, he gave her the low-down on the neurochemistry of positive feedback. "Positive comments will produce other 'happy' chemicals in our bodies," he explained. "The 'happy chemicals' are known as EDSO (endorphins, dopamine, serotonin and oxytocin). These chemicals, when properly balanced, enable us to function to our full potential.

"Endorphins block pain and enable us to 'power through' to reach a goal. Think of a 'runner's high'. Dopamine is the goal-setting chemical, enabling us to focus on an end result and producing the thrill of accomplishment when it is reached. Serotonin is the selfless response we feel as pride, especially valuable in that it encourages us to push hard to make those who sacrifice for us proud. This encourages leaders to sacrifice for the good of the group, and the group to strive to please the leader. We are not drawn to selfish leaders, but to those who appreciate and acknowledge the work that others do to help them reach their goals.

"Oxytocin is love, friendship, hope and joy. It is the happiness we get when we are able to perform an act of generosity with no expectation of receiving something in return. Oxytocin is also produced by human contact; it is why we shake hands and pat each other on the back. People

---

52 http://www.gallup.com/businessjournal/182321/employees-lot-managers.aspx

with more oxytocin are better problem solvers, are healthier and live longer."

That's the kind of biological power you're tapping into when you praise - so why wouldn't you praise as much as humanly possible?

My favourite quote about the power of praise in action comes from Julia, a senior leader in a large telco we worked with. "All of our meetings used to start with 'f**ks', " she said. "Oh f-this, f-that". Now we start every meeting with 'Thanks'. " Everyone in Julia's meetings now starts by thanking someone in the room for something they've done that day or week. It may be surprising, but it's so emotional and genuine. Also hilarious.

From f**ks to thanks: we were very tempted to make that the title of this book.

BUZZ MEETINGS

A 'buzz meeting' is a first-thing get-together intended to set your team up for success for the day and remind them to, in everything they do, put people first. Remember our 'eyes up' morning brain hack above? That's a perfect example of a buzz meeting. It's more than just a vehicle to impart information and energise the team; it's an opportunity to uncoach multiple people at a time in an inspiring way. 'Hello, ROE!'

So don't just pile on the scatter-gun whoops and high-fives. Get specific. Is there one thing that all the team could be better at? What one small thing will they all focus on today, to make a big difference? To make it feel effortless, put in some sneaky planning time before you leave work the night before. Read through the uncoaching techniques that follow and test them out; buzz meetings are the perfect time to practise some ESP, priming or head boosting (see more on these below). Also, remember to use the concepts above. So feed the pig by focusing on inputs, not outputs. Praise publicly, and encourage your people to praise each other (thanks not f**ks).

Buzz meetings are also a good opportunity to try out the 'moodometer'. This is a fun tool used by organisations such as Nordstrom People Lab[53] and inspired by some interesting psychological science suggesting that, by keeping track of what you do and how happy you feel, you can have more happiness more often. All you have to do is draw a scale with different emotions on it, ranging from angry to frustrated to bored to neutral to hopeful to happy (you can get creative here) on flipchart paper and ask people to make a mark on the scale to represent how they're feeling as they walk in. You can then track the changes and patterns and use your insights as a regular buzz meeting discussion point.

A warning, though: you have to commit to making your buzz meeting the highlight of everyone's day. A limp buzz meeting is worse than no buzz meeting at all. At one mobile network provider we worked with, their managers claimed to have run out of things to do in a week. It showed that we still had some serious work to do on imagination mindset! Even worse was the utilities company that used all their fifteen-minute buzz meetings to do a general knowledge quiz. A little bit of me died inside every morning when I had to endure it, and a bit more died as I walked past every single team doing the same thing.

That's not it. That's s**t. Don't be s**t. Be an amazing leader who people will talk about for years after they've retired.

TECHNIQUES: EXPLORE, SHOW AND PRACTISE

ESP is the big daddy of uncoaching techniques.

It goes like this. Pick a behaviour or mindset you want to explore. Now ask the person you're with what they already know about it, and how they'd rate their current ability. Then show them how to do it through role play, with you taking their part and them playing the customer. Demonstrate what good sounds like and let them hear the difference.

---

53 https://peoplelabdev.wordpress.com/research/moodometer/

Finally, switch the roles, with you playing the customer and them playing themselves.

Why is ESP so important? Well, if the ultimate goal of your uncoaching is to make the customer conversations in your organisations feel more present, human and connected, you'd better, um, have some actual conversations, for real. You want your people to get better at something? You'd damn well better help them hear and taste and feel what better looks like in practice.

Unfortunately, as soon as you utter the words "role play" people come out in cold sweats. It somehow makes them think of traumatic times in their school drama class. So, don't mention role play. Talk about practising instead. Make it quick and easy. Do it all the time. Be casual and upbeat about it. Just make sure that you're uncoaching by getting your people to say words, not getting them to listen to you.

It can be handy here to build a best practice conversation library, allowing you to discuss parts of other conversations and practise different responses. Give your team the best practice code. Again, but be sure to emphasise that this is not a test. It's a safe, supportive practice in which you can both feel free to play, make mistakes and feed that growth mindset.

Now go out there and do it.

YOU'RE AWESOME

Pick a person on your team. Reflect deeply on what they are good at. Listen into their next conversation and note all the good things they say, then go and tell them these things... and only these things. Be specific. Be positive. Be enthusiastic. Be grateful. Be sincere. Then be quiet, and walk away.

This small exercise will be so worth it; your subject might initially be suspicious, but they'll soon realise there's no sting in the tail, and they'll feel incredibly valued. More of the good stuff will show up every day.

If doing this makes you feel a bit, well, icky, it only goes to serve as proof of the extent to which we hate giving praise (particularly in the UK). Get over it. It'll make you feel brilliant, too.

AFTER THE FACT

This technique is great if you are short on time or if you've discovered that you love to 'walk and talk'. The essence of it is that you don't always have to hear what's going on in a conversation to be able to add value.

Simply go up to one of your team and ask them to tell you about a great conversation they've had that day. This is the best question that anybody in the business can ask, whether you work in marketing or you're the CEO. This is the mother of all hacks - we're talking tone, we're talking climate, we're talking every conversation in the business. The best single way to crack the conversation code in your climate is to ask your people to tell you about a great conversation they've had that day. It'll not just encourage them to reflect on the choices they made, it'll give you insight into how they talk about themselves, what they consider great and how easy they find it to be positive. It'll encourage you to stay curious. And it'll make a perfect little story for you to share more widely.

ROE alert.

PRIMING

We've already explored the science about priming but, as a quick reminder, it's "a nonconscious form of human memory concerned with perceptual identification of words and objects, which refers to activating particular representations or associations in memory just before carrying out an action or task."[54]

In human speak, it's the technique of using certain words and images to influence people to behave in a certain way. It sounds creepy. It's not. It's totally transparent and actually very simple. It means that as your team

---

54 https://www.psychologytoday.com/basics/priming

arrives for work, focused on the horrible commute they've just had, you can help shift their mindset by using positive language and imagery.

Try this in your buzz meetings. Say people a lot. Say customer a lot. Say real a lot. Figure out your own favourite keywords. Project a strong supporting image on the meeting room screen, or rip it out of a magazine, or show them on your phone. And share a couple of your latest positive stories to remind them what you're aiming for.

HEAD BOOST

As we discussed in Chapter 5, no-one's at the top of their game all the time. Tiredness, germs, iPad-obsessed kids at home, too many carbs at lunch... So, it's important to have a technique up your sleeve that will help you to inject some instant energy and motivation into those who need it most.

Be present. Look around. Who looks like they are down, fed up, low, flat and could do with a head boost? Go over. Ask a casual, non-pressured 'What's up?' Show empathy and support. Use the techniques of 'you're awesome', 'after the fact' and 'priming' to nudge them into a better place.

A change of scenery can also do wonders. If you can, give them a break or go for a quick 'walk and talk'. The brisker the better - oxygen really, really helps.

JFDI

Find someone who's struggling and tell them, in a no-nonsense tone, to "Just f***king do it".

No, don't. Seriously. Never do this. This is not coaching. This is not uncoaching. This is called being a dick.

NEXT CONVERSATION

Sometimes, you come across someone in your team who has a lot of different things they need to work on, or a new starter with an awful lot to learn. This can feel a bit overwhelming for them, and as an uncoach it can be hard to know where to start. That's when you reach for the 'next conversation' technique. This will give you both razor sharp clarity and focus on what's going to happen next.

You simply say "What I would like you to do on your next conversation is..."

Let them have the conversation and then report back on how it went (or listen in to see how it goes). Congratulate them and acknowledge them for doing it ('you're awesome'). Then get them to do it on the next five conversations and report back to you; then on the next ten conversations; then on every conversation for the day. Until they are just doing it, and don't need to report back to you anymore.

Achieving one clear success like this will really motivate them to tackle the next change. It's also an example of the 'small change, big difference' concept we explored above. When it comes to uncoaching, you can't expect instant results - you have to keep plugging away, shifting mind-sets a tiny bit in each session, until the behaviour finally clicks.

JFKG (Just f**king keep going). That was another frontrunner for the title of this book.

CONCLUSION: THE BIG BAD WOLF

We believe that, with the right input, most people can shift their output. By applying the concepts, methods and techniques above, you will be helping customer-first behaviours to show up across the business and most people will be thriving.

Most. Because in real life, not all stories have happy endings. Sometimes, people just don't want to become the hero of their own fairytale. Despite your best, brilliant uncoaching efforts, some people want to stay stuck as a minor character, repeating their same old ineffectual behaviours and mindsets again and again.

This is where we find most managers get stuck too, because they don't know what to do. When you've tried everything to no avail, the time comes when you have to have the uncomfortable conversation, the WTF dude conversation - I call it the fierce conversation - but most of us shy away.

However, fierce conversations are not the big bad wolves we mentally make them out to be. They're just another conversation. And whenever you arrive at a conversation you know you need to have but you don't want to have, there's a simple tool you can use to help you out. It's literally as simple as ABC:

- A is for agenda: make sure everything you do is about making things more human
- B is for behaviour: stay focused on people's actions, not their identities
- C is for curiosity: remember that there are always multiple ways of looking at things

This ABC works for any fierce conversation, personal and professional. I'm going to finish this chapter by handing back to Sally, who claims that this tool saved her marriage. I'll let her explain…

I work full-time while my partner stays at home looking after our three beautiful children (the ones who squabble, spend all their time on inappropriate devices and are often also naughty in restaurants). Every evening, when I'd get back home, I'd find that my partner had cooked dinner for the kids, but hadn't left any for me.

After a while, as I travelled back home on the train every evening, I'd start to tell myself stories in my head: I'm so hungry, I'm starving, he won't have left me any dinner, why does he feed the kids and not me, if roles were reversed I'd be expected to put dinner on the table, he doesn't care, he resents me for working... and so on. It's amazing how the stories you tell yourself about a situation can build emotion around it before you've even got there.

So, there I would be, on the way home, getting more and more angry in my own mind. I'd ring the doorbell and this big bad wolf would come to the door, all innocent, and say "Hi!" And the first thing I'd say, without so much as a hello, was "What's for dinner?" - with an edge to my voice. That edge had intent. The intent of that edge was to prove that there wasn't any dinner. To prove me right.

"Dinner?" he'd say, with an edge, because he'd picked up on my edge. And the evening would go from there (imagine away).

Let's use ABC to pick this apart.

In any conversation that is probably going to cause contention, you need to be really clear on your intent. What's the agenda? Why are you bringing this conversation to the table? Do you want to help, to make the relationship with this person better... or do you just want to be right? This is an incredibly common dynamic, at work as well as at home, and one of the biggest mistakes we make in fierce conversations is being unclear about what we really want from having it. So, that's A: making sure you have your agenda straight.

As for B, the key here is to remember that there's a massive difference between somebody's identity and their behaviours. When I found out there was (yet again) no dinner, I would say something like "You're lazy" - a statement that would instantly cause a problem because that would go straight to my partner's identity, making him feel like he was being attacked as a person and inevitably leading to a defensive attitude. A statement like "I'd love it if you'd put a little bit more energy into that", focusing on what he did and not who he was, would have allowed both of us to be much more calm and rational. So B simply means: keep it about behaviour, not identity.

Finally, C asks you to bring in that old curiosity mindset, with undertones of flex. It's surprisingly tough to accept that there are two sides to every story: that your view of the world will always be different to someone else's. Just because someone hasn't done the thing that you want them to do, doesn't mean that there aren't reasons you might be oblivious to. So, reminding yourself that you might not have all the information about a situation is essential if you're going to avoid our old enemy: assumption.

When I finally got fed up with our evening stand-offs, rather than spending my commute making up stories about how s**t my partner was, I reflected on how I could try a more ABC tack. First I said hi, and took my coat off, and waited until we were inside with a glass of wine. Then I began with A: "I want to have a conversation, because there is something that has been bothering me, and if I don't say it, it's going to bother me for longer, and I want to find out what's been going on for you." Then I moved on to B: "What I've really noticed is that you seem to cook supper for the kids but there is never any left for me, that has me thinking... (that you don't give a s**t about me? NO, SALLY! C, C, C!)... er, why are you doing that? What's going on for you? Because what that feels for me is that you're not giving me any thought. Is that right?"

And of course, he said, "Oh...well... I never even thought about it!" Which deflated all my anger, made me realise that he was coming from a totally different point of view, and allowed us to have a real, human conversation with a productive outcome (he cooked a bit extra for me).

So, ABC works brilliantly for both routine uncoaching conversations and fierce conversations. But it also works really well in any situation where there's a rising elephant.

I'll use one final story to illustrate what I mean.

A few weeks ago, I was sat in a meeting where everyone in the room was talking frankly about how difficult they found a particular company process. Then the most senior person in the organisation came in. One guy chose to raise the topic and before he'd even stopped talking it became very obvious that this was going to become a contentious issue. Suddenly, everybody's heads went down. They were all incredibly interested in their hands or their laps. Nobody supported this guy and boom! There it was - a massive, leathery, smelly elephant, rising in the room. Our daring guy was left exposed, and now there was this elephant that everyone was trying their very hardest not to look at.

So, a rising elephant is a conversation that badly needs to happen and never does. It happens all the time. I bet you can identify a few recent meetings or conversations which have been conducted around the stamping feet of a rising elephant.

But with ABC, even the un-discussable can be discussed. It gives you a clear and safe three-step strategy to ensure that your conversation will remain calm, impersonal, positive and focused on productive outcomes. Before you know it, your elephant will have become a mouse.

If you learn your ABC and use the methods and techniques above, I guarantee you'll be surprised about how good an 'uncoach' you already are. As Steve says, it's just another set of conversations, after all.

 CRUNCH TIME: TEST YOUR UNCOACHING

Dedicate some time to a company-wide walkabout, taking a different circuit of your building, store or office. If you work out in the field, spend a few days shadowing your team. Count how many managers have their 'eyes up' and spend time having conversations with a random selection of people you come across in your travels, either recording them on your phone or - if that feels intrusive - pausing after each one to make a few notes. Ask each of them two questions:

- What three things did you do brilliantly?
- What small change do you think would make a big difference?

This is a simple way to take the temperature of your climate, but it's remarkably accurate. You can create some hard data out of it - an average 'eyes up' score, the ratio of positive to negative stories, which behaviours are weakest and which mindsets are strong. But it will also help you get a real, intuitive, human feeling for your organisation's tone.

Is this a flourishing, positive, self-aware company that puts people first? How do you feel after hearing these conversations? What was the quality of those conversations? Are you bouncing out of the organisation with a grin on your face or sitting on the train, telling angry stories in your head?

If your managers are uncoaching several times every day, your front line staff are having better and better conversations, and elephants are being pointed out as soon as they rise up, then it's time to move onto our final chapter, and ask yourself the single big question at the heart of this book.

>_ SOURCE CODE: CHAPTER 7

- You don't have to be a 'master coach' to transform your team's performance dial - for many managers that is a big ask which is likely doomed to fail.
- Instead what we need is a wave of managers who encourage, stimulate, invigorate, tickle, inspire, nudge their people to become the best version of themselves. Uncoaching is about catching people doing things right, keeping your eyes up, encouraging the seven behaviours to show up and tapping into people's motivations. It is just another conversation, and it only take minutes to make a difference.
- Feed the pig: the numbers will not shift by simply watching them. Managers have to focus on the inputs (behaviours) that will crack the code.
- Think SCBD: focusing on small changes in behaviours will make a big difference on performance and will ensure you get a high ROE (Return on Energy).
- There are many easy, energising, uncoaching methods and techniques you can use: from walk the walk, to ESP, to You're Awesome - just get stuck in.
- Focusing on the positive does not mean you shy away from challenging discussions. In fact, these are just another conversation and they can be easy as ABC…

CHAPTER 8: WHAT ARE YOU FOR?

HARD CHOICES

It's time to revisit the question with which we began this book. Despite all the science and knowledge out there, all the insight on mindsets and behaviours, why do just a select handful of companies consistently ace customer experience, while everyone else still struggles to bring it to life? What exactly is that 'magic bullet' that separates the best from the rest?

In a 2014 TED Talk that has been viewed by 4.5 million people,[55] the philosopher Ruth Chang offers advice on how to make 'hard choices'. Which career should I pursue? Should I break up or get married? Where should I live? Big decisions like these can feel painfully difficult, and Chang suggests that lists of pros and cons won't help.

Hard choices are hard, she explains, when both options have good and bad points, but neither is better overall. - nor are they equally good; if so we could simply flip a coin. Instead, hard choices are hard because they rely on a fourth, less 'tangible' factor than concepts such as better, worse or equal. They rely on our beliefs about who we are.

"When we choose between options that are on a par, we can do something really rather remarkable," Chang insists. "We can put our very selves behind an option. Here's where I stand. Here's who I am, I am for banking. I am for chocolate donuts. This response in hard choices is a rational response, but it's not dictated by reasons given to us. Rather, it's supported by reasons created by us. When we create reasons for ourselves to become this kind of person rather than that, we wholeheartedly become the people that we are."

Hard choices don't tend to crop up that often for us in our personal lives because, by the time we reach adulthood, we have largely internalised 'what we're for'.

---

55 https://www.ted.com/talks/ruth_chang_how_to_make_hard_choices/transcript?language=en#t-93023

Take conversation. When we talk to others we make a string of choices in terms of the tone we adopt, the words we use, the questions we do or don't ask. But those choices are usually easy, even invisible. We rarely agonise about how to gossip with our best friend, help our children with their homework or interact with a waiter in a restaurant, because our unconscious preferences guide our speech.

When you work in delivering customer experience, it's different. People on the sales and service frontline have to make hundreds of hard choices every day. Every time they talk to a customer, they must consciously shape the conversation on behalf of the business. And although they always know what they want - to sell that product, or solve that problem - they rarely understand 'who they are' as they attempt to do it, or which of their instincts they can trust. The result is either a stilted, inflexible and 'inhuman' exchange that falters when it inevitably veers off-script, or a wildly inconsistent range of responses as someone attempts to square their personal values with their professional obligations.

The gap between their natural desire to have a real conversation, and what they are expected to do in their job, is just too big. That's the gap into which all the good intentions fall.

The same goes for conversations across the organisation itself. From the way a manager signs off emails, to the questions the Head of HR asks a new recruit, a company's 'voice' is defined by all the collective conversations had by its people, day to day - and the result is often a dissonant mess.

WHAT ARE YOU FOR?

An organisation's 'character' is a shared project. The people inside it, at every level, must repeatedly have conversations that reiterate the essence of what it is - and what it is not. But it is only when they understand its ethos and behaviours as deeply and instinctively as their own that their conversations will stop being buggy algorithms full of hard choices and start to become effortlessly effective, individually nuanced and deeply human experiences.

So, it's time for you to make the hard choice at the heart of this book: are you ready to crack the code? In other words, are you willing to do the day-to-day work it takes to create a climate where customer experience can thrive, starting right now, one conversation at a time?

I truly believe that if you set the right tone, create a climate of permission, train for new behaviours, embed resourceful mindsets and uncoach every day, you can create an organisation that delights customers, engages its workforce and delivers market-leading financial results. I believe it because I've seen it happen.

But it only happens when - and this is the crunch point - the leaders of that organisation are absolutely committed to making it work. When they make it their job to do all those things first, more creatively, more consistently and more visibly than anyone else, every single day. When they make it the one vital priority of their job to tell stories and have conversations, above writing reports and answering emails and filing expenses and even making coffee.

And that takes us right back where we started, to my son and his damn iPad.

HAPPY EVER AFTER...ISH

It was only a few months ago that I finally decided that our miniature evening cycle of frustration, irritation, guilt and disappointment had to stop. The next time my son was badgering us all to help him with the iPad, I took a long hard look at the behaviour going on in the 'front line' of my very own living room.

Who, out of this group of human beings, was having a good conversation? No-one. My older kids were retreating into circle 1, getting more introverted the more their brother nagged. I was going to the opposite extreme, pushing my own agenda, finding a way to stop him from hassling me without ever really pausing to ask him what he wanted or why. Like your average CEO, I thought the fix was a technological one, when it wasn't. Our cure was conversational.

Together, we'd created a climate of disempowerment. My kids were sending the message: you're less important to us than our devices. I was sending the message: just let me solve this problem for you, and be quiet. And as one of the theoretical 'leaders' of this family, I wasn't exactly role-modelling great behaviour, either: I was multitasking, obsessing over technology and prioritising my evening 'process' over the needs of the living, breathing members of my family in the room. Over the past few weeks, I'd been sitting on my favourite rung of the accountability ladder, 'Waiting and hoping': hoping that my partner would come up with a superior parenting strategy, or maybe even that Apple might launch some app to make iPads toddler-proof.

What my son wanted, of course, was attention. Equipped with a growth mindset, he didn't want me to solve the problem for him; he wanted me to help him figure it out himself. He also had a bunch of other needs and wants I hadn't bothered to explore, which were making him even more impatient than usual (he hadn't had much lunch and was hungry, for one).

So, in that moment, I made a decision which is what this book is all about: being present in every conversation in my own house. For the first time, I really, properly realised that everything that I talk about at work applies at home, and that the happiness of my family life lay in making every single conversation count. Making a conscious choice to be present with the impact of your conversations every day

The upshot is that we've broken the cycle of iPad rage in our house (most of the time). Even better, my favourite presence circles have become a sort of emotional shorthand in our house. When I hear my youngest nagging and nagging away at the others upstairs, I nip into the hall and shout "Circle 2!" (at which point my partner Richard will roll his eyes and say "God help them!").

Except we really don't have to say it as much as we used to, anymore. Because they're real, the lessons in this book. They don't just apply to leadership or organisational dynamics or customer experience.

They apply to any situation that involves conversations. So, after all those years spent developing, refining and practising them in a professional context, I'm now trying to spend more time having better ones in my personal life. It's hard. I'm very far from perfect (very far). But I'll tell you something.

I know I'll crack it eventually, because I'm taking it one conversation at a time.

ACKNOWLEDGEMENTS

Writing the book was easy (see first acknowledgement). Writing the acknowledgements page has been comparatively a great deal more difficult. I googled (when did that become a verb?) 'how to write book acknowledgements' and discovered there are two ends of a very broad spectrum; at one end, the authors who see the acknowledgements page as a life award acceptance speech, thanking everyone with whom they have had a conversation since birth; at the other end, those who just stick to thanking the people who directly helped in the writing of the book. I chose to operate at the latter end, mostly for fear of missing someone out. If you were expecting to be on the acknowledgements page and have arrived here to discover you are not, this one's for you. Thank you. You are awesome.

So, to the first acknowledgement - Molly Flatt; you write like I wish I could; with the humour, I wish I could articulate; with a humility I wish I could find; and with a mannerism that had my mother believe I wrote every word. You have turned my 25 years of stories, experiences and insights into a coherent, eloquent and persuasive read. I could not be more proud of this book and so I thank you with an excitable squeeze that says this book is everything I have imagined it could be for the many years I have been itching to write it.

To Sean Spurgin and Steve Bent, my co-authors and partners in crime - for having the patience of saints when, having declared my nonchalance to the specific content of a chapter, I proceeded to debate every sentence. For all the laugh-out-loud moments - there will always be BOFO. But mostly for your brilliant contribution and a conveyer belt of continually evolving ideas that keep us dangling over the cutting edge.

To Andy Moorhouse, our very own Blue Sky Boffin, without whom we have no ninjas, a blueprint is just for architects and diagnostic objectives are confined to the pages of our operations handbook. You are our official in-house genius and this book has reaped the benefit of your provocative and disruptive insights.

To the whole of the Blue Sky team - my one-woman mission to change the nation's service turned into an army of tempered radicals inspiring a revolution that makes the world just a little bit more human. You all inspire me to be the best I can be every single day.

To Caroline Bird - without you, quite simply, there would be no book. To Marc Jantzen, whose leadership example still guides my thinking and my actions and to Miranda Cain, whose counsel keeps me sane and everyone else safe.

To my kids - you get the smallest slice of my time, but the biggest slice of my heart. I hope that, despite my absence from home, my evangelistic passion for work inspires you to follow your dreams, do what you love and achieve any 'big hairy goal' you set yourself (even writing a book).

To Richard, for making sure at least one parent is present at the important events and for putting up with ladders on the fridge; and finally, to mum, for your constant source of positive energy and pride.

OK, so maybe more like a life award acceptance speech then!

APPENDIX

FLEX QUESTIONNAIRE

Each question offers four statements: A, B, C and D. Score the statement that describes your behaviour the most with a 4, the next with a 3, then 2 and finally the statement that describes your behaviour the least with a 1. You cannot score different answers with the same number, so the total score for each question should always add up to 10.

Before you start, remember:

- It's not about you; it's about identifying how to flex yourself for the customer.
- There are no right or wrong answers.
- Think about your actual behaviour, not how you would like your behaviour to be perceived by others.
- Don't take too long on each question; gut feeling is usually the most accurate.
- You might find it easier to score the statement that best describes you first (allocating a 4), then the statement that least describes you next (allocating a 1) and then decide on the two in the middle (allocating a 2 then 3).

Question 1: I like...
A. To make decisions quickly and get on with it.
B. To know where everything is and have everything organised.
C. To be considerate of others, treating them as I would expect to be treated.
D. To experiment with different ideas. If it sounds good, I'm happy to give it a go.

Question 2: When completing a task, I like...
A. To achieve the results and meet targets.
B. To ensure I have clarity and detail and everything is factually correct.
C. To create a bond with others and take their thoughts into consideration.
D. To have variety, be creative and have fun.

Question 3: When thinking about work...

A. I know what I want and strive to achieve it with little fuss.

B. I like to work in a quiet environment that allows me to think in a systematic and logical way.

C. I want to be of value to a team, ensuring I do my utmost to help others.

D. I like to have a great team of people around me who I can bounce ideas off.

Question 4: I consider myself to be...

A. A daring person who is willing to take risks and push the boundaries.

B. An objective and practical person who does not make rash decisions.

C. A considerate person who is loyal and trustworthy.

D. An engaging person who is spontaneous and flexible.

Question 5: When in a learning environment, I like...

A. To have clear actions and purpose, with not too much small talk and silly activities.

B. To fully understand the information, ask lots of questions and seek clarity.

C. To have discussions in smaller groups and not be asked to stand up and present to the whole group.

D. For it to be lively, with lots of engaging activities and games.

Question 6: In a group environment I will usually...

A. Say what I'm thinking, be ready for action and tend to take the lead.

B. Be more reflective, ask questions and strive to generate order and structure.

C. Think things through before saying them out loud and ensure that everyone has their say.

D. Be very talkative, not always thinking things through, but always liking to be involved.

Question 7: People can sometimes perceive me as...

A. Unmovable; if I think it's right then it's right.

B. Too concerned with structure, process and detail.

C. A soft touch and worrying about others.

D. Unfocused, disorganised and easily distracted.

Question 8: One of my strongest qualities is...

A. I have very high standards; I like achieving results and getting things done.

B. I have a wealth of information and rarely get things wrong.

C. I have a caring nature and devote time to others.

D. I am an optimistic person who looks at the positive side of the situation.

Question 9: When planning an activity...

A. I take a limited brief and take immediate action.

B. I study the facts carefully before deciding on the correct course of action.

C. I involve others and obtain different opinions.

D. I play around with different ideas and eventually get started.

Question 10: When under slight pressure, I can...

A. Become very demanding of others.

B. Become rigid in my thinking and won't deviate from a process.

C. Become stubborn, worried and dig my heels in.

D. Become unable to make a decision, not knowing what to start first.

Question 11: My desk would be described as...

A. Functional - I have everything I need to hand.

B. Extremely tidy with everything in its place.

C. Calm with a family photo or two.

D. A mess - is there a computer under there somewhere?

Question 12: I like others to...

A. Be clear, concise and tell me what I need to know.

B. Give me all the information, facts and timescales and be logical in the way they communicate.

C. Take into consideration my feelings and demonstrate they value my opinions and care.

D. Be spontaneous, fun and sociable.

Now calculate your total scores for A, B, C and D. A is your score as a Competitive Driver, B is your score as a Logical Analyser, C is your score as a Loyal Connector, and D is your score as a Creative Enthusiast. Your highest two scores indicate your dominant preferences, and your lowest two scores indicate your least dominant preferences.

FLEX TYPES

Logical Analysers

Logical Analysers are great organisers who seek to control the world around them with structure and discipline. They take time to do the job right, are organised, focused and will check and recheck information to ensure it is accurate. They thrive in environments where systems and procedures are clearly defined and they enjoy working with detail and facts. Calm, reflective, detail-conscious and planned, are adjectives that describe people of this preference. Structure, goals and clear deadlines motivate these people. Information and data needs to be understood and digested before they are willing to extrovert their ideas and contribution. They believe in fairness- what is right, not who is right. They seek order and accuracy, to ensure they provide the perfect solution. Being introverted they can be viewed by other preferences as quiet and non-emotional. Also, their reflection and drive to cross Ts and dot Is, can slow down the decision-making process and ultimately the completion of a task.

Competitive Drivers

Competitive Drivers are confident and get the job done. They are great at anything that requires a rapid response. They know what they want and go after it, even when there is opposition. They take on the challenge and love to be around people who share their desire to achieve and be successful. They thrive in a fast-paced environment where the purpose is clear and there are plenty of opportunities to excel. They are direct, objective driven, risk takers and completers. People with this preference strive to reach goals at all times. What is the goal? what are the milestones? and what does success look like? are constant questions and behaviours that people of this preference extrovert. They like a degree of control and can often be the individuals that take the lead in discussions, or decision making. Being more extroverted, they tend to express their point of view and are not frightened to challenge others with different views. They need to be aware, that their drive for achievement can come across as aggressive or opinionated to other preferences. They also need to ensure that their desire to reach goals does not encourage them to make decisions too quickly, or with a lack of detailed information.